HISTORY AND GEOGRAPHY 1105
A NATION DIVIDED AND UNITED

CONTENTS

Author: **Alpha Omega Staff**

Editor: Alan Christopherson M. S.

Illustrations: Alpha Omega Staff

Alpha Omega Publications®

804 N. 2nd Ave. E., Rock Rapids, IA 51246-1759
© MM by Alpha Omega Publications, Inc.   All rights reserved.
LIFEPAC is a registered trademark of Alpha Omega Publications, Inc.

HISTORY 1105
A NATION DIVIDED

During the years after the War of 1812, the population of the United States increased rapidly. Industry expanded, agricultural production boomed, settlers began to move into new territories, roads and canals were constructed over mountains and through dense forests, and the cry of "Manifest Destiny" could be heard across the nation.

Manifest Destiny was the idea that the citizens of the United States had a God-given right to extend their way of life from the Atlantic to the Pacific and that no physical barrier or human force could stop the settlement of these lands. This idea became a prevalent thought in the minds of many United States citizens. The expansion into new territories across the continent was a direct link in the chain of events leading to the Civil War.

Each time new territory was acquired by the United States, the troublesome question of slavery was raised. Many people in the anti-slavery faction of the North and West persisted in thinking that slavery in the territories would result in the economic superiority of the South and the demise of free enterprise. The proslavery faction, in contrast, feared the destruction of the "Southern lifestyle" unless the balance between free states and slave states could be maintained.

The increase in universal white male suffrage was another factor that helped create the sectionalism that paved the way for the war. After the Declaration of Independence, state laws in the thirteen states stipulated that only white men with considerable property or those who paid high taxes were allowed to vote. These laws were still in effect after the War of 1812. Between 1816 and 1821 six new states were admitted to the Union that allowed all white men to vote without regard for property qualifications. With the addition of these new states, the eastern and southern states began to relax their voting restrictions, many men who had never shown an interest in politics began to participate in the elective process. For the first time the "common" man had the opportunity of electing people to office who would encourage the federal government to adopt policies primarily beneficial to his sectional needs.

In the years following the War of 1812, the United States extended its boundaries from the Atlantic coast to the Pacific coast. With this expansion came issues that divided one section of the nation from another. As the United States grew, the way of life changed from one section to another. Southern living, for example, was entirely different from that of the West or Northeast.

In this unit you will study the conditions of life in the East, the West, and the South. You will also study the Civil War and the reconstruction efforts after the war.

OBJECTIVES

Read these objectives. The objectives tell you what you will be able to do when you have successfully completed this LIFEPAC®. Each section will list according to the numbers below what objectives will be met in that section.

When you have finished this LIFEPAC, you should be able to:

1. Describe the physical and sociological features of the South, the West, and the Northeast.
2. Define issues which caused the polarization of the nation prior to the Civil War.
3. Review both the Northern and the Southern views of these issues.
4. Identify the leading personalities of the Civil War era and explain the consequences of their actions.
5. Identify generalizations about the effect of slavery on owners and slaves.
6. Define the strengths and weaknesses each side possessed in facing the Civil War.
7. Identify major battles of the war and how each victory or defeat contributed to the outcome of the war.
8. Outline effects of the war on the North and the South.
9. Examine the reconstruction efforts made after the Civil War.
10. Recognize that God is no respecter of persons and that we are all equal in His sight.

Survey the LIFEPAC. Ask yourself some questions about this study. Write your questions here.

_____

_____

_____

_____

_____

_____

_____

_____

_____

_____

_____

I. REGIONAL LIFESTYLES

In this section and the next you will examine the prewar lifestyles of three regions and see how these differences in lifestyle contributed to sectionalism and the problems that followed.

SECTION OBJECTIVES

Review these objectives. When you have completed this section, you should be able to:

1. Describe the physical and sociological features of the South, the West, and the Northeast.
2. Define issues which caused the polarization of the nation prior to the Civil War.
3. Review both the Northern and the Southern views of these issues.

VOCABULARY

Study these words to enhance your learning success in this section.

agrarian	Organized or designed to promote agricultural interests
artisan	One trained in some mechanical art or trade
drainage basin	A land drained by a river and its tributaries
fall line	Place where rivers descend in falls or rivers from a piedmont to a plain
growing season	The period between the last killing frost in the spring and the first killing frost in the fall
piedmont	Hilly land at the foot of mountains
sod	Soil filled with the roots of grass, herbs, and so forth

Note: All vocabulary words in this LIFEPAC appear in **boldface** print the first time they are used. If you are unsure of the meaning when you are reading, study the definitions given.

REGIONAL LIFESTYLES: THE EAST AND WEST

Life in the East. In 1850 more than half of the factories in the United States were located in the Northeast with two-thirds of the nation's production value centered in that region. The Northeast was unsuitable for large-scale farming because of the mountainous terrain and the short **growing season**—only three months in some places. However, the rough, rocky mountains with rivers coursing down their sides were an ideal source for the power necessary to run the machinery in the new mills and factories of the budding Northeastern textile industry. They also had a ready source of cotton in the south.

Because the growing season was short and the hard, rocky ground kept agricultural production near the subsistence level, more people lived in the cities of the Northeast to find work than in either the West or the South.

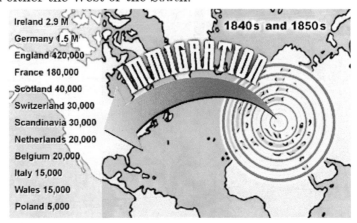

Ireland 2.9 M
Germany 1.5 M
England 420,000
France 180,000
Scotland 40,000
Switzerland 30,000
Scandinavia 30,000
Netherlands 20,000
Belgium 20,000
Italy 15,000
Wales 15,000
Poland 5,000

IMMIGRATION   1840s and 1850s

In the years preceding the Civil War, a new wave of immigrants came to the United States, fleeing the potato famine of 1845 and 1846 in Ireland. A few of the immigrants remained in the southern entry ports of Charleston and New Orleans. However, the majority swelled the numbers in the northern cities where they found work in the factories. By 1857 the number of factory workers had risen to 1.2 million, and the industrial labor force to almost 1 million people working an average of sixty-eight to seventy-two hours a week.

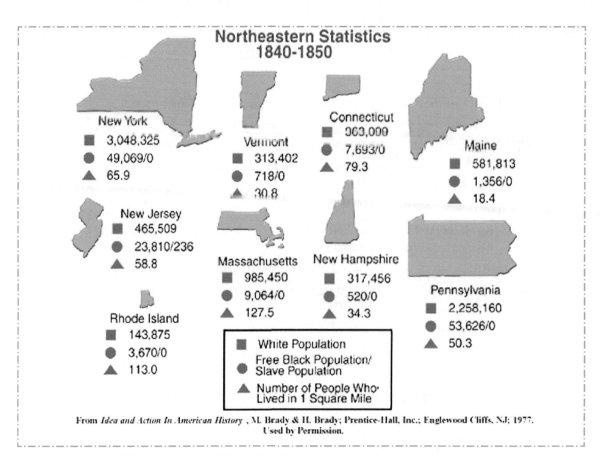

Northeastern Statistics
1840-1850

New York
- ■ 3,048,325
- ● 49,069/0
- ▲ 65.9

Vermont
- ■ 313,402
- ● 718/0
- ▲ 30.8

Connecticut
- ■ 363,099
- ● 7,693/0
- ▲ 79.3

Maine
- ■ 581,813
- ● 1,356/0
- ▲ 18.4

New Jersey
- ■ 465,509
- ● 23,810/236
- ▲ 58.8

Massachusetts
- ■ 985,450
- ● 9,064/0
- ▲ 127.5

New Hampshire
- ■ 317,456
- ● 520/0
- ▲ 34.3

Pennsylvania
- ■ 2,258,160
- ● 53,626/0
- ▲ 50.3

Rhode Island
- ■ 143,875
- ● 3,670/0
- ▲ 113.0

- ■ White Population
- ● Free Black Population/ Slave Population
- ▲ Number of People Who Lived in 1 Square Mile

From *Idea and Action In American History* , M. Brady & H. Brady; Prentice-Hall, Inc.; Englewood Cliffs, NJ; 1977.
Used by Permission.

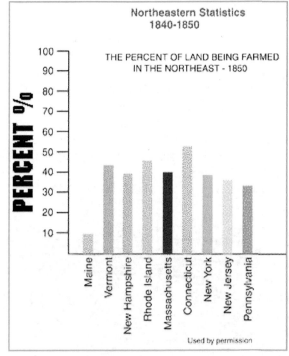

Northeastern Statistics
1840-1850

THE PERCENT OF LAND BEING FARMED IN THE NORTHEAST - 1850

Used by permission

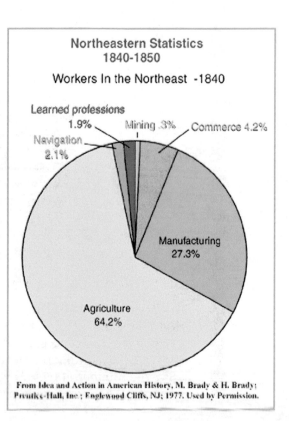

Northeastern Statistics
1840-1850

Workers In the Northeast -1840

- Learned professions 1.9%
- Mining .3%
- Commerce 4.2%
- Navigation 2.1%
- Manufacturing 27.3%
- Agriculture 64.2%

From Idea and Action in American History, M. Brady & H. Brady;
Prentice-Hall, Inc ; Englewood Cliffs, NJ; 1977. Used by Permission.

4

City workers developed machines and products to make their lives easier. Charles Goodyear's vulcanized rubber was patented in 1844 and was used for boots and shoes. Elias Howe's sewing machine was patented in 1846. The telegraph was patented by Samuel Morse in 1862 and increased intercontinental communications. These inventions are examples of some of the machines and products of the period.

The major cities of the Northeast—Philadelphia, Trenton, New York, Buffalo, Hartford, Providence, and Boston—had cobblestone streets, gas lanterns posted on brick or flagstone sidewalks, and gutters that ran down the middle or sides of the streets carrying the sewage. The more enlightened cities had street cleaners, watchmen who handled thieves and looters, and chief engineers who coordinated the efforts of volunteer firemen. The shops of small **artisans**, merchants, cabinetmakers, silversmiths, candle makers, blacksmiths, clock makers, milliners, printers, and grocers lined the streets. Horse-drawn carriages rumbled across the cobblestones while hawkers called out, selling water, milk, wood for fuel, fruit, and hot foods such as boiled corn and gingerbread. Other peddlers bought rags, old metal, and rope.

Brick or board houses lined the streets of the residential areas, and a few public and religious schools and academies were available for those who were able to pay tuition. Tenement houses became home for some factory workers; other factories provided small houses near the plant for their laborers. Black freedmen and Indians lived in the cities of the North. They ran small businesses, were service workers in homes and inns, and worked in the factories like other common people of the time.

Wealthy merchants and industrial capitalists wielded vast political power because of their great wealth. The general public tended to agree with their political and industrial leaders, whatever their own social or economic class. During that period, the people of the Northeast became more concerned about the needs of those around them. Most of the great reform movements flowered in this region of the country. The demand for public education, prison reform, assistance for the physically handicapped, care for the insane, women's rights, temperance, ideal societies, and **abolition** all found support in that region. The Northeast favored governmental aid to business, the protective tariff, and controlled bank credit. It did not, however, favor westward expansion, especially if it included slavery.

Study the statistics of the Northeastern states in the figure on the previous page and fill in the blanks.

1.1   The largest Northeastern state was _____ with a white population of _____ people.

1.2   The smallest Northeastern state was _____ with a white population of _____ people.

1.3   The most densely populated state was _____ with _____ people per square mile.

1.4   The state with the highest percentage of land being farmed was _____.

1.5   In Maine only _____ percent of the land was used for farming.

Match the countries with the number of immigrants.

1.6   _____ Ireland   a. 420,000

1.7   _____ Germany   b. 180,000

1.8   _____ Poland   c. 15,000

1.9   _____ France   d. 2,900,000

1.10   _____ Belgium   e. 5,000

1.11   _____ England   f. 20,000

1.12   _____ Italy   g. 1,500,000

 Complete this map activity.

1.13   Write the numbers of the cities listed below at their correct location on the map.

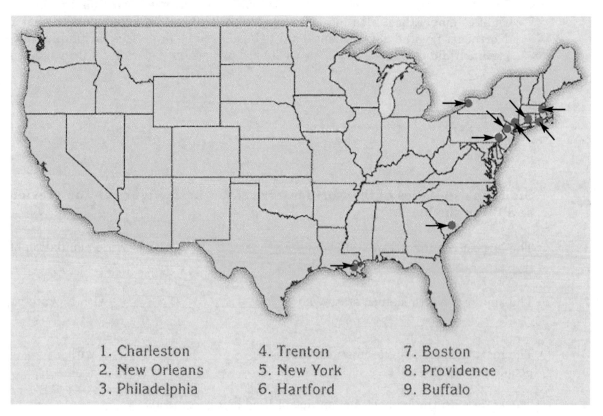

1. Charleston   4. Trenton   7. Boston
2. New Orleans   5. New York   8. Providence
3. Philadelphia   6. Hartford   9. Buffalo

Choose the correct answer(s).

1.14   Two emerging factors after the War of 1812 that contributed to development of sectionalism
were:
_____   a. the stricter voting laws
_____   b. the demise of free enterprise
_____   c. an increase in the number of men voting
_____   d. a rapid decrease in the population of the United States
_____   e. the concept of Manifest Destiny

Match following vocabulary words with their definitions.

1.15   _____ abolitionist   a. the period between the last killing frost in the spring
                                       and the first killing frost in the fall

1.16   _____ artisan   b. soil filled with the roots of grass, herbs, and so forth

1.17   _____ drainage basin   c. one trained in some mechanic art of trade

1.18   _____ growing season   d. a person who wants to do away with some rule of custom

1.19   _____ sod   e. a land drained by a river and its tributaries

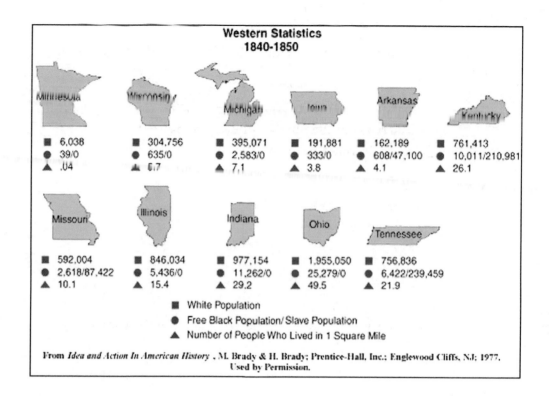

Western Statistics
1840-1850

Minnesota	**Wisconsin**	**Michigan**	**Iowa**	**Arkansas**	**Kentucky**
■ 6,038	■ 304,756	■ 395,071	■ 191,881	■ 162,189	■ 761,413
● 39/0	● 635/0	● 2,583/0	● 333/0	● 608/47,100	● 10,011/210,981
▲ .04	▲ 5.7	▲ 7.1	▲ 3.8	▲ 4.1	▲ 26.1
Missouri	**Illinois**	**Indiana**	**Ohio**	**Tennessee**	
■ 592,004	■ 846,034	■ 977,154	■ 1,955,050	■ 756,836	
● 2,618/87,422	● 5,436/0	● 11,262/0	● 25,279/0	● 6,422/239,459	
▲ 10.1	▲ 15.4	▲ 29.2	▲ 49.5	▲ 21.9	

■ White Population
● Free Black Population/ Slave Population
▲ Number of People Who Lived in 1 Square Mile

From *Idea and Action In American History* , M. Brady & H. Brady; Prentice-Hall, Inc.; Englewood Cliffs, N.J; 1977. Used by Permission.

Life in the West. In 1860 the West covered three vast natural regions. The first of these natural regions ran from the interior plains of Ohio and Indiana west to Iowa and north to Wisconsin and Minnesota. The second region included the Pacific coast states of California and Oregon. The third natural region included the unorganized area gained during the Mexican War and the Rocky Mountain region.

The interior plains are the home of the great rivers and lakes of the United States. The mighty Mississippi River (originating at Lake Itasca in Minnesota), the Missouri River, the Ohio River, and the land surrounding them form the great **drainage basin** that ends at New Orleans and the Gulf of Mexico.

The rich fertile soil of this region, with a growing season of five to seven months and flat terrain, encouraged the development of large family-type farms. These farms were generally cultivated using new farm machinery and equipment. The use of the efficient McCormick reaper, patented in 1824 by Cyrus McCormick, was one of the reasons why western farmers did not need to rely on a large number of people for human labor. Because the new threshers, rakes, and seed drills were made of iron and later steel, the demand for these products in the West caused the iron industry in the East to expand.

The western farm family, with the help of a few hired hands during harvest, produced a surplus crop of corn, rye, wheat, oats, beans, and potatoes and developed a lively trade with the eastern industrial region. They raised large herds of cattle or sheep farther north, where the growing season was much shorter, and in the arid southwest part of the region.

The temperature of the interior plains region fluctuates greatly between winter and summer. The winters are extremely cold, as low as twenty-three degrees below zero in some places and the summer temperatures can soar as high as 100 to 105 degrees F. The vast flat area of the plain is subject to arctic breezes and endures winds from the south during the late summer months that sometimes end in tornadoes.

Early homes in the West were often log cabins built from the trees that were felled to clear the land for farming. On the open prairie where no trees grew, houses were made of **sod** until boards could be transported from the East. Tents and wagons served as temporary homes for the settlers that trekked across the Rockies to Oregon or California.

The coastal and Sierra Nevada mountain ranges in California and the Cascade range in Oregon surround a central valley that was fertile and well protected from ocean winds. The climate in the central valley of California is mild; temperatures do not vary greatly between summer and winter months.

The mountains of California and the Rocky Mountain territories yielded precious metals that attracted miners and other adventurers to this area. In the dry inter-mountain region, the newcomers met an already flourishing culture and adopted the dry-farming methods of the Indians and Mexicans of this area.

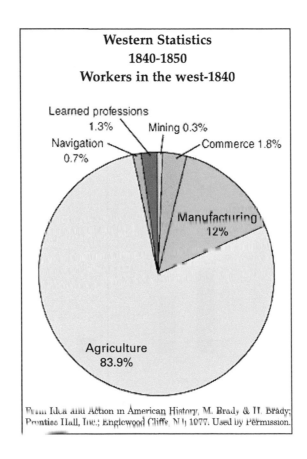

Western Statistics
1840-1850
Workers in the west-1840

Learned professions 1.3%
Mining 0.3%
Navigation 0.7%
Commerce 1.8%
Manufacturing 12%
Agriculture 83.9%

From Idea and Action in American History, M. Brady & H. Brady; Prentice Hall, Inc.; Englewood Cliffs, NJ; 1977. Used by Permission.

Many people traveled to the West by stagecoach. They boarded the stage in St. Louis and rode three weeks across Texas, New Mexico, and Arizona territory to California. In 1861 travelers on the Overland Trail caught fleeting glimpses of the riders on the pony express as they whizzed by.

Many immigrants found their way to the West, where land was cheap and in some places immigrants formed the majority of the people in the area. The West attracted people who were adventurous and saw that area as a land of opportunity. There, they did not encounter the rigid class distinctions of the East and the South. Practically all white men owned property and were able to vote in the West. Westerners became proud of the fact that no permanent class of laborers existed and that each man had the opportunity of advancing to property ownership.

The cities of the West were the fastest growing cities in the nation. In 1850 the population of Chicago stood at thirty thousand people, and in less than six years that number had almost tripled. Located at the tip of Lake Michigan, Chicago became the nation's largest railroad center and ultimately became the trade center of the West, with easy access to the Mississippi, the port of New Orleans, and across the Great Lakes route through the Erie Canal to the East coast.

Western Statistics
1840-1850

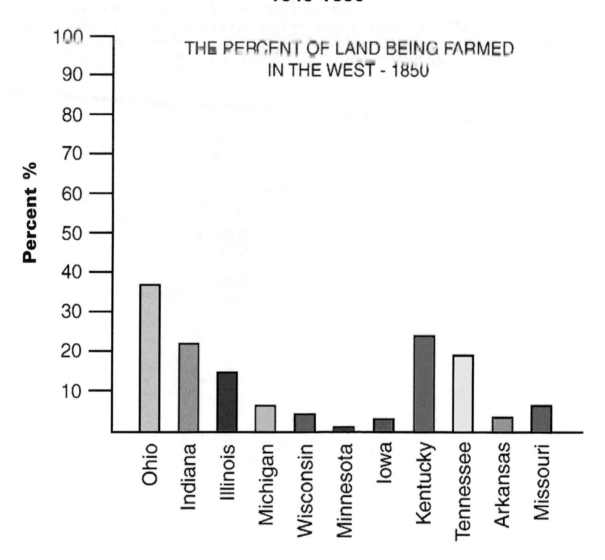

THE PERCENT OF LAND BEING FARMED
IN THE WEST - 1850

Percent % (y-axis: 10, 20, 30, 40, 50, 60, 70, 80, 90, 100)

States (x-axis): Ohio, Indiana, Illinois, Michigan, Wisconsin, Minnesota, Iowa, Kentucky, Tennessee, Arkansas, Missouri

In Ohio many farmers raised large herds of swine, and in the cities pigs ran through the streets as scavengers of the sewage. Soon Cincinnati became known as the nation's pork packing center.

On the outer fringes of the West, the people clustered around forts. At first, the forts served as protection from the Indians. As the Indians were forcibly removed to reservations, the forts became the social and trade centers of the area. The frontier had receded from the Atlantic coast in the 1600s to the prairies and the intermountain region by 1850.

The people of the West wanted internal improvements financed by the federal government, cheap or free public land, and easy bank credit. The West drew closer to the East as transportation lines to the East coast made trade with this region accessible and profitable.

Small numbers of free blacks lived in the Northwest and far West, riding the ranges, prospecting for minerals, and leading settlers across the western trails to the Pacific coast. The people of the West opposed slavery—some because they did not want to compete with slave labor in the territories and others because they saw slavery as a demeaning system harmful to the master as well as the slave.

Choose the correct answer.

1.20   The Mississippi River begins at Lake:
_____ a. Erie.
_____ b. Itasca.
_____ c. Superior.
_____ d. Winnibigoshish.

1.21   The growing season in the interior plains lasts how many months?
_____ a. five to seven
_____ b. four to six
_____ c. five to six
_____ d. three to five

1.22   The reaper was invented by:
_____ a. Cyrus Field.
_____ b. James Howe.
_____ c. Eli Whitney.
_____ d. Cyrus McCormick.

1.23   Homes on the prairies were built out of:
_____ a. logs.
_____ b. sod
_____ c. boards.
_____ d. bricks.

1.24   The fertile central valley is located in:
_____ a. California.
_____ b. Oregon.
_____ c. Arizona.
_____ d. Washington.

1.25   The nation's largest railroad center was located in:
_____ a. Cincinnati.
_____ b. Kansas City.
_____ c. Chicago.
_____ d. New York.

1.26   The nation's pork-packing center was located in:
_____ a. Cincinnati.
_____ b. Kansas City.
_____ c. Chicago.
_____ d. New York.

Study the statistics of the Western states and fill in the blanks.

1.27   The four western states that were slave states were _____ ,
        _____ , _____ , and _____ .

1.28   The total Western white population from 1840 to 1850 was _____ people.

1.29   The most populous Western state was _____ with a white population of
        _____ people.

1.30   The Western state with the largest free black population was _____ .

1.31   The Western state with the largest slave population was _____ .

1.32   The Western state with the fewest people per square mile was _____ .

True/False.

1.33   _____   About 37 percent of Ohio's land was used for farming.

1.34   _____   Minnesota had more land in agriculture than any state.

1.35   _____   Agriculture accounted for more workers in the West than any other occupation.

1.36   _____   Manufacturing accounted for 12 percent of the workers.

Complete this map activity.

1.37   Write the numbers of the cities listed below at their correct location on the map.

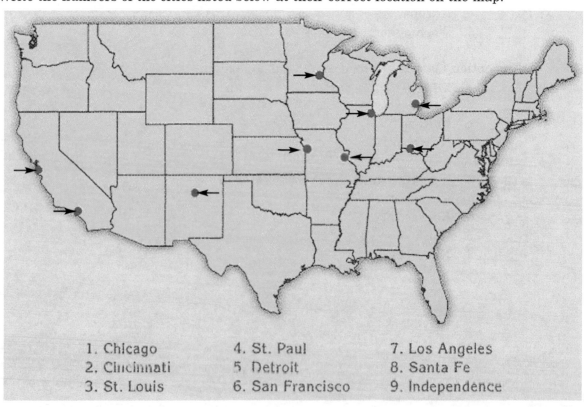

1. Chicago	4. St. Paul	7. Los Angeles
2. Cincinnati	5. Detroit	8. Santa Fe
3. St. Louis	6. San Francisco	9. Independence

12

REGIONAL LIFESTYLES: THE SOUTH

Slavery was at the center of the Southern economy. The relationship between slaves and owners not only affected the economy and individuals but also all the social institutions of the region.

Life in the South. The plantation system of assigning vast property in land and slaves elevated a few men to positions of superior power, financially and socially. Furthermore, the isolation of plantations and farms led to family relationships on neighboring properties. The sons and daughters of wealthy planters often married the sons and daughters of the neighboring planters. The resultant lines of kinship that included cousins, aunts, and uncles tied many people together across miles and miles of territory. This feature of Southern sociology probably accounts for the fact that the great majority of Southern officers in the United States armed forces—who were drawn by more than just the ideal of Southern independence—resigned their commissions, sadly turned their back on the Union, and joined forces with other men from their states when secession became an accomplished fact.

The classes of Southern whites were not often in conflict. The plantation produced a staple crop which was usually sold on the international market. The small farmer had the opportunity of selling his own truck crops, livestock, and grain to the plantation as well as to the city dwellers. The Southern farmer was not in competition with the plantation, but was a service worker for it. He derived economic benefits from the institution. Manufacturing and commercial enterprises were also direct beneficiaries of the plantation system and slave labor. The white Southerners were drawn together by the common need to "manage" the slaves and freedmen for the good of the "Southern way of life."

The isolation of the rural South led to the development of an individualism that focused on personal and local needs. Southerners saw a parallel between the South and the colonies of 1776. Southerners believed their rights under the Constitution were threatened. They believed their culture was different and superior to the North, and they were determined to assert their independence.

In the North many people believed the South should be allowed to become an independent country. Other people, however, talked about the long border existing between the Confederacy and the North and suggested that trouble could continue for many years. They pointed out that trade between the two countries could be impeded and that the people of the United States had been one nation for almost one hundred years. The fact that a large portion of productive land and taxable property would be lost, as well as free access to the mouth of the Mississippi River for midwestern agricultural products, must certainly have played a part in the North's desire to keep the South in the Union.

The natural regions of the South include the coastal plains, the **piedmont** plateau, the peaks and valleys of the Allegheny, the Blue Ridge ranges of the Appalachian mountains, the Bluegrass region of Kentucky, the interior plains of the South, the swamps of the gulf, the Ozarks, and the dry lands at the edge of the prairie in Texas.

The Atlantic and Gulf coastal plains formed the farming regions of the South. Precipitation and high temperatures produced the humidity that encouraged tropical growth in some areas. Here, the first settlers found dense forests and numerous rivers. These natural resources provided abundant fish and game and enabled the Southerners to develop an inexpensive transportation system, by water, to the export centers along the coast.

In 1850 the South was the most rural and **agrarian** of all the regions in the United States, producing cotton, tobacco, rice, sugar, and hemp. Most of the people lived on small farms or plantations. Many of the city dwellers were employed in commerce that was a direct result of slave labor.

Southern Statistics
1840-1850

Workers In the South-1840

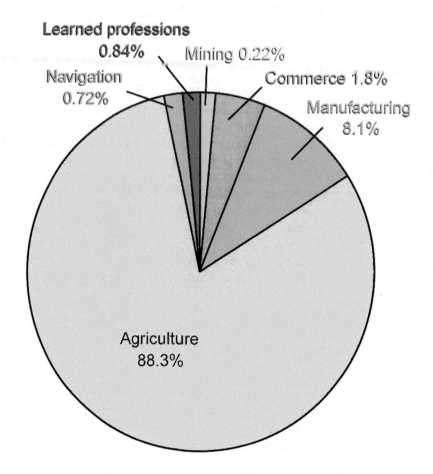

From *Idea and Action in American History*, M. Brady & H. Brady; Prentice-Hall, Inc.; Englewood Cliffs, NJ; 1977. Used by Permission.

The South was divided into two regions, the Old South and the Lower South. The Old South had grown rice, indigo, and tobacco for years until the soil was depleted. The Old South included the states of Maryland, Delaware, Virginia, North Carolina, South Carolina, and Georgia. The Lower South, west of the Appalachians and bordering the Gulf, was the land of cotton and sugar.

Many of the homes of the wealthy planters in the Old South were palatial, but most of the people lived in plain board or brick houses. West of the Appalachians, before the install-ment of sawmills, the houses were often log cabins. Frederick Law Olmstead, a Northerner traveling through the south in the early 1850s, described the farms of the poor as log cabins with one room and another separate cabin which served as a kitchen. Each farm had a well for water and a small enclosed garden. Those farmers had an abundance of cows, goats, mules, and hogs, in addition to wild game.

Although primarily rural, the South had a number of prominent cities. West of the Atlantic coastal plains at the foot of the Appalachian mountains, the great inland cities of Montgomery, Columbus, Macon, Augusta, Columbia, Raleigh, Richmond, Fredericksburg, Washington, D.C., and Baltimore developed. These **fall line** cities utilized water power derived from the nearby rivers that tumbled from the higher Appalachians to the floor of the Atlantic or Gulf coastal plains.

Atlanta, Georgia, one of the greatest cities in the South, developed at the terminus of railroad lines that were laid around the Appalachians. Richmond, Virginia, the region's most industrial city, was the nation's tobacco center. New Orleans, the largest city of the Lower South, was the most pluralistic city of the region. The French heritage was retained, and many of the European immigrants who stayed in the South settled in New Orleans. New Orleans' location at the mouth of the Mississippi assured its prosperity. Cotton from the South and agricultural products from the Northwest were shipped from New Orleans. Imports from Europe, Latin America, and Asia were unloaded in this busy commercial center.

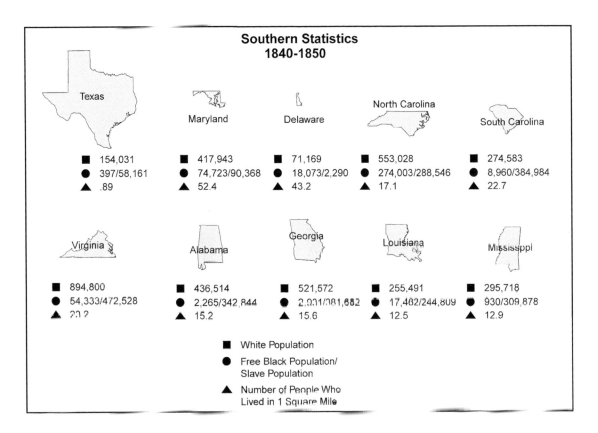

Southern Statistics
1840-1850

Texas	**Maryland**	**Delaware**	**North Carolina**	**South Carolina**
■ 154,031	■ 417,943	■ 71,169	■ 553,028	■ 274,583
● 397/58,161	● 74,723/90,368	● 18,073/2,290	● 274,003/288,546	● 8,960/384,984
▲ .89	▲ 52.4	▲ 43.2	▲ 17.1	▲ 22.7
Virginia	**Alabama**	**Georgia**	**Louisiana**	**Mississippi**
■ 894,800	■ 436,514	■ 521,572	■ 255,491	■ 295,718
● 54,333/472,528	● 2,265/342,844	● 2,931/381,682	● 17,462/244,809	● 930/309,878
▲ 20.2	▲ 15.2	▲ 15.6	▲ 12.5	▲ 12.9

■ White Population
● Free Black Population/
Slave Population
▲ Number of People Who
Lived in 1 Square Mile

Charleston, South Carolina, long considered the "capital" of the south, was the fifth largest city in the nation in 1810. Although the population in the city doubled between the years of 1820 and 1869, Charleston declined in rank because of the relative growth of the other urban areas in the North and West. By 1860 Charleston ranked as the twenty-second city in the United States.

The class structure of the South was dominated by the planters (the men who owned ten or more slaves), the cotton kings, and the tobacco magnates. The trained professionals, including doctors, lawyers, teachers, and the clergy, were next in the hierarchy. The small independent farmers, merchants, and white artisans were placed above the poor. The poor lived in the hills and swamps on depleted land, subsisting largely on fish and game. The poor and the slaves were at the bottom of the class scale.

The "peculiar institution" (slavery) was the overriding circumstance that separated the South from the remainder of the nation. Slavery held the South in bondage to an archaic way of life. By 1860 slavery had reached its height after some two centuries of growth. Only 383,637 were slave-holders out of a total white population of over eight million. Some 2 million persons, however, were connected with slavery either by family connections or by direct interest. Three-fourths of the white population in the South were in no way connected with slavery. Of the 383,637 slave holders, only 48,566 held twenty or more slaves. When a plantation had twenty or more slaves, an overseer was needed. One-half of the slave holders owned less than five slaves, and nearly one-third owned only one or two slaves—generally a black family, a domestic, an artisan, or a field hand.

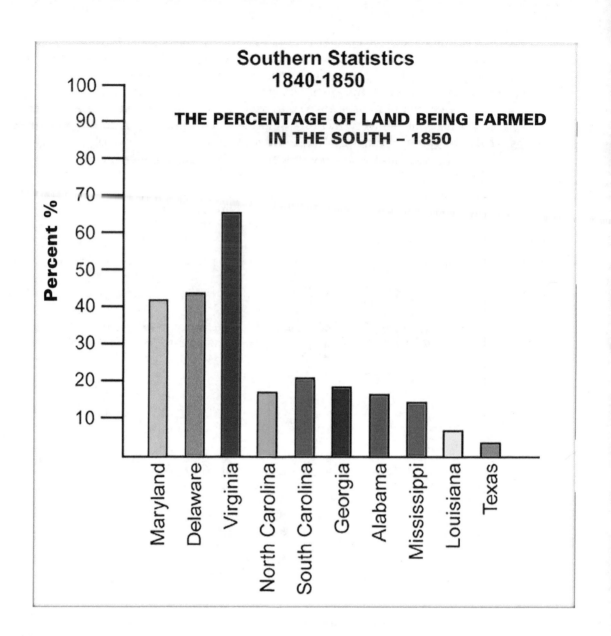

Southern Statistics
1840-1850

THE PERCENTAGE OF LAND BEING FARMED IN THE SOUTH – 1850

Three important factors influenced the Southern lifestyle: (1) the gentleman planter and his lifestyle, (2) the hot and humid Southern weather with dry summers and occasional winter frosts, and (3) the black slaves. By 1860 the black population was 4,215,614 out of a total population of over 12 million in the South.

Match these vocabulary words with their proper meanings.

1.38 _____ agrarian

a. hilly land at the foot of mountains

1.39 _____ fall line

b. organized or designed to promote agricultural interests

1.40 _____ piedmont

c. place where rivers descend in falls or rivers from a piedmont to a plain

Choose one answer.

1.41 What did many Northern people believe about the South?

_____ a. that its economic focus should become industrial rather than agricultural.

_____ b. that Manifest Destiny did not apply.

_____ c. that it should close Southern ports to midwestern shippers.

_____ d. that it should be allowed to become an independent country.

Study the statistics of the Southern states and fill in the blanks.

1.42 The total slave population was _____ .

1.43 The total slave population of Tennessee, Arkansas, Missouri, and Kentucky was

_____ .

1.44 The total slave population of the slave states was _____ .

1.45 The state with the largest slave population was _____ .

1.46 The state with the fewest people per square mile was _____ and the

state with the greatest population density was _____ .

1.47 The slave state with more free black people than slaves was _____ .

1.48 The major occupation of the South was _____ .

1.49 By 1850 six items being produced by the South were :

_____ , _____ , _____ , _____ ,

_____ , and _____ .

1.50 The six states included in the Old South were:

_____ , _____ , _____ ,

_____ , _____ , and _____ .

17

Complete this map activity.

1.51   Write the numbers of the cities listed below at their correct location on the map.

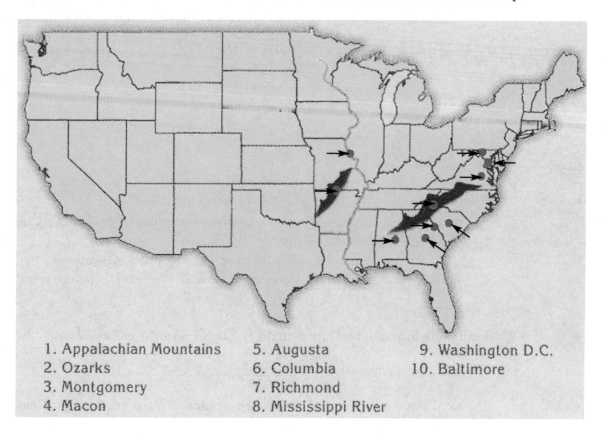

1. Appalachian Mountains 5. Augusta   9. Washington D.C.
2. Ozarks   6. Columbia   10. Baltimore
3. Montgomery   7. Richmond
4. Macon   8. Mississippi River

Adult Check   _____

        Initial   **Date**

Review the material in this section in preparation for the Self Test. The Self Test will check your mastery of this particular section. The items missed on this Self Test will indicate specific areas where restudy is needed for mastery.

SELF TEST 1

Match these items with their proper descriptions (each answer, 2 points).

1.01 _____ Manifest Destiny   a. the southern state with more free Blacks than slaves

1.02 _____ Ireland   b. someone who wants to do away with some rule or custom

1.03 _____ abolitionist   c. right to all land from the Atlantic to the Pacific

1.04 _____ Cyrus McCormick   d. 2,900,000 immigrants to United States

1.05 _____ Northeast   e. reaper

1.06 _____ Delaware   f. had more than half the factories in 1850

1.07 _____ Lake Itasca   g. most densely-populated state in the North

1.08 _____ Chicago   h. capital of the South

1.09 _____ Cincinnati   i. beginning of the Mississippi River

1.010 _____ cotton   j. pork-packing center

1.011 _____ Massachusetts   k. largest railroad center

1.012 _____ Charleston   l. most important crop in South

Match these vocabulary words with their proper meanings (each answer, 11 points).

1.013 _____ agrarian   a. a land drained by a river and its tributaries

1.014 _____ fall line   b. soil filled with the roots of grass, herbs, and so forth

1.015 _____ piedmont   c. one trained in some mechanic art or trade

1.016 _____ abolitionist   d. the period between the last killing frost in the spring and the first killing frost in the fall

1.017 _____ artisan   e. a person who wants to do away with some rule or custom

1.018 _____ drainage basin   f. place where rivers descend in falls or rivers from a piedmont to a plain

1.019 _____ growing season   g. organized or designed to promote agricultural interests

1.020 _____ sod   h. hilly land at the foot of mountains

Choose the best answer(s) (each answer, 2 points).

1.021   Three resources available to New England textile manufacturers were:
      _____ a. power from waterfalls
      _____ b. government grants
      _____ c. labor
      _____ d. canals
      _____ e. cotton from the South

1.022   The telegraph was invented by:
      _____ a. Elias Howe.
      _____ b. Samuel Morse.
      _____ c. Charles Goodyear.
      _____ d. Cyrus McCormick.

1.023   The dry, treeless region that lies between the Mississippi River and the Rocky Mountains is called the:
      _____ a. Central Valley.
      _____ b. fall line.
      _____ c. Great Plains.
      _____ d. piedmont.

1.024   How long is the growing season in the interior plains?
      _____ a. five to seven months
      _____ b. four to six months
      _____ c. five to six months
      _____ d. three to five months

1.025   The reaper was invented by:
      _____ a. Cyrus Field.
      _____ b. James Howe.
      _____ c. Eli Whitney.
      _____ d. Cyrus McCormick.

1.026   Homes on the prairies were built out of:
      _____ a. logs.
      _____ b. sod.
      _____ c. boards.
      _____ d. bricks.

1.027   The fertile central valley is located in:
      _____ a. California.
      _____ b. Oregon.
      _____ c. Arizona.
      _____ d. Washington.

1.028   Small southern farmers:
      _____ a. did not support slavery.
      _____ b. competed with the plantations.
      _____ c. sold their food crops to the plantations.
      _____ d. sold their crops to Northeastern cities.

1.029   In 1850 the fastest growing cities were in the:
_____   a. west.
_____   b. south.
_____   c. northeast.
_____   d. southwest.

True/False (each answer, 2 points).

1.030   _____   Practically all white men in the West owned property and were allowed to vote.

1.031   _____   A large majority of the white population of the South owned slaves.

II. CIVIL WAR

A civil war, a war between peoples of the same country, is a terrible human tragedy. A conflict of this kind rages more fiercely than any other, and its flames are slower to die out. A civil war leaves deep, ugly scars on the nation, no matter who wins or loses.

In the early 1850s few people believed that the United States would ever undergo such an ordeal as a civil war. The United States had seemed divinely blessed. The borders of the United States reached from the Atlantic Ocean to the Pacific Ocean and from Canada to Mexico, enclosing some of the most beautiful land on earth. The standard of living was rising, and thousands of immigrants were flocking to the United States seeking a better way of life.

Beneath the surface of all this prosperity, however, the deep roots of sectionalism were having a tremendous effect on the nation. Although the North and South had been able to reach compromises on many of their disagreements, they had failed to settle some important differences. As these differences became great, increasing distrust resulted, frustration grew, and emotion instead of reason began to govern.

Finally, in 1861 civil war replaced the political art of compromise. The nation's future was in the hands of armies. War raged bitterly for four years with tremendous loss of lives on both sides. Before the guns fell silent, Northerners and Southerners were joined together in the firm resolve which Lincoln uttered in behalf of all citizens of the United States: "That this nation, under God, shall have a new birth of freedom—and that government of the people, by the people, for the people, shall not perish from the earth."

In this section we shall examine the Civil War from the first shots fired at Fort Sumter to the surrender at Appomattox, Virginia.

SECTION OBJECTIVES

Review these objectives. When you have completed this section, you should be able to:

4. Identify the leading personalities of the Civil War era, and explain the consequences of their actions.

6. Define the strengths and weaknesses each side possessed in facing the Civil War.

7. Identify major battles of the war and how each victory or defeat contributed to the outcome of the war.

10. Recognize that God is no respecter of persons and that we are all equal in His sight.

VOCABULARY

Study this word to enhance your learning success in this section.

    specie   Money in the form of coins; metal money

CIVIL WAR: DIVISION AND ANTAGONISM

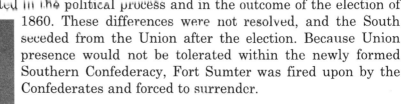

The Division. The ability to work out a compromise on a difficult issue is often thwarted by the demands of the vested interests and the pride of both sides. The sectional differences in the country were reflected in the political process and in the outcome of the election of 1860. These differences were not resolved, and the South seceded from the Union after the election. Because Union presence would not be tolerated within the newly formed Southern Confederacy, Fort Sumter was fired upon by the Confederates and forced to surrender.

Sectional politics emerge. The Democratic national convention met in Charleston, South Carolina, in April 1860. Stephen Douglas hoped to be nominated but was disappointed when Southerners, who wanted the right to take their property into all territories, refused to vote for him unless he changed his stand on popular sovereignty. This refusal eventually led to a split in the Democratic party.

Stephen Douglas

The Democratic convention adjourned without a candidate. It reconvened in June, nominating Douglas without the cooperation of the Southern delegates, who walked out of the convention again. The Southern Democrats later nominated John Breckinridge of Kentucky on a platform that supported the federal protection of slavery in the territories.

William H. Seward

The Republican delegates met in Chicago in May. They agreed that, because of the split in the Democratic party, a Republican victory was probable if they selected the "right" candidate.

The contenders for the nomination were Salmon P. Chase of Ohio, Abraham Lincoln of Illinois, and William H. Seward of New York. Seward was the best known of the three, but he had gained a reputation of being stubborn when he had referred to the "irrepressible conflict" in describing the sectional differences plaguing the nation. Abraham Lincoln, who expressed more moderate views on slavery, was nominated on the third ballot. The Republicans tried to temper Southern opposition to Lincoln by denouncing John Brown's raid and by upholding the Fugitive Slave Law of 1850.

The Republican platform opposed the extension of slavery into the territories but withheld interference with slavery in the states where it already existed. The platform approved the protective tariff, federal funding for river and harbor improvements, and free western land. It also favored building the transcontinental railroad across the northern route.

The fourth candidate to run for the presidential office was John Bell of Tennessee. Bell's Constitutional Union Party supported the Constitution, the preservation of the Union, and enforcement of the law. The deletion of any reference to slavery from Bell's platform was an obvious attempt to appease voters on both sides of the Mason-Dixon line.

John Bell

Abraham Lincoln was elected with less than 40 percent of the popular vote. He won the 180 electoral votes of all the free states except New Jersey, which gave him the electoral majority. Breckinridge, the Southern Democratic candidate, carried all the states of the lower South, with Maryland and Delaware, for seventy-two electoral votes. The candidates of the parties that ran on a compromise platform received the fewest electoral votes. Bell gained thirty-nine votes from Kentucky, Tennessee, and Virginia; and Douglas received twelve votes from Missouri.

The South Secedes. South Carolina called a state convention in December of 1860, little more than a month after the election. The convention voted to repeal the state's ratification of the Constitution and to formally secede from the Union. Political leaders in other states urged their constituents to wait and give the Lincoln administration the opportunity to show whether it would indeed enforce the Fugitive Slave Law and conform to other Southern demands. Both Sam Houston and Jefferson Davis tried to delay secession, but they were unsuccessful against the organized extremists who called for the separation of the Union.

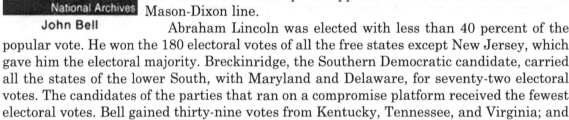

THE SOUTH SECEDES

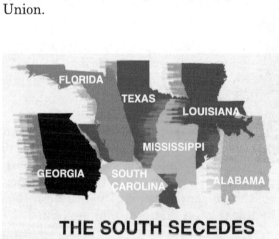

Abraham Lincoln

By February of 1861, six more states — Mississippi, Florida, Alabama, Georgia, Louisiana, and Texas — had seceded from the Union. The arguments that made secession attractive to some Southerners included three proposals: (1) the end of the tariff that benefited the North and penalized the South, (2) the possibility of reopening the slave trade, and (3) the possible annexation of Cuba, Santo Domingo or Mexico for the extension of the plantation system.

Most Southerners did not think that the North would fight to keep the unhappy South in the Union. If war did erupt, the people in the South felt that their victory would be assisted by proslavery factions in the North and by the European governments that needed cotton for their economy.

President Buchanan was still in office when the six Southern states seceded. He declared that secession was unconstitutional but that Congress had no power to use force against a state. Instead of calling loyal citizens to support the Union, Buchanan urged compromise with Southern demands.

Senator John J. Crittenden of Kentucky proposed a set of Constitutional amendments to ensure the maintenance of the Union. His suggestions included: (1) extending to California the Missouri Compromise ban on slavery north of the 36°30' parallel, (2) guaranteeing federal protection of slavery south of this line, (3) supporting popular sovereignty for all future states, (4) vigorously enforcing the Fugitive Slave Law and reimbursing owners for unrecovered fugitive slaves, and (5) insuring for posterity that Congress could not interfere with slavery in any state or in the District of Columbia.

Twenty-one states, led by Virginia, made a second compromise effort. The peace convention made proposals similar to the Crittenden compromise that had been defeated by Congress two months earlier. This effort, too, was defeated.

On the same day that the peace convention was making suggestions for a compromise, the seceding states met in Montgomery, Alabama and formed the Confederate States of America. They adopted the "stars and bars" as their flag, elected Jefferson Davis as their president and Alexander H. Stephens of Georgia as their vice president, and drafted a constitution.

President Jefferson Davis

**Vice President
Alexander H. Stephens**

The Confederate constitution was similar to that of the United States but included passages that restrained the new government from passing laws that interfered with slavery, initiated protective tariffs, or appropriated funds for internal improvements. The Confederacy made immediate military plans and captured a number of federal forts, custom houses, and post offices throughout the South in defiance of Buchanan's threat of military force to meet such confiscation.

After the six deep-South states seceded, the people in the upper South — Virginia, Maryland, North Carolina, and Delaware — and those in the border states of Tennessee, Kentucky, Arkansas, and Missouri were embroiled in bitter controversy. The decision to remain with the Union or to join the Confederacy divided neighborhoods and families.

Lincoln's inaugural address, delivered in March of 1861, made clear that he would enforce the federal regulations and assist in returning fugitive slaves to all states. Lincoln implied that he would not resist a constitutional amendment guaranteeing no interference with the existing institutions in the states, including slavery. Lincoln also stressed his obligation to maintain the Union, stating his intention to "hold, occupy, and possess the property and places belonging to the Government and to collect the duties and imposts" in all the ports. He declared that the future of the country rested with the South. "In your hands,

March 4, 1861

Fellow citizens of the United States:

In compliance with a custom as old as the government itself, I appear before you to address you briefly, and to take, in your presence, the oath prescribed by the Constitution of the United States, to be taken by the President "before he enters on the execution of his office."

I do not consider it necessary, at present, for me to discuss those matter of administration: about which there is no special anxiety, or excitement.

my dissatisfied fellow-countrymen and not in mine is the momentous issue of civil war ... You have no oath registered in heaven to destroy the government, while I shall have the most solemn one to preserve, protect and defend it." He then added this famous statement:

> "...I am not loath to close. We are not enemies, but friends. We must not be enemies. Though passion may have strained it must not break our bonds of affection. The mystic chords of memory, stretching from every battlefield and patriot grave to every living heart and hearthstone all over this broad land, will yet swell the chorus of the Union when again touched, as surely they will be, by the better angels of our nature."

Fort Sumter

Fort Sumter falls. Lincoln urged the people of the Union to reflect before acting to secede. "My countrymen, one and all, think calmly and well upon this whole subject. Nothing valuable can be lost by taking time. If there be an object to hurry any of you in hot haste to a step which you would never take deliberately, that object will be frustrated by taking time; but no good object can be frustrated by it."

The day following his inauguration, Lincoln received a message from Major Robert Anderson at Fort Sumter in the Charleston harbor. Anderson reported that he could not remain in control of the fort without the assistance of added troops and without provisions for his island-bound men. Lincoln had pledged to hold all federal property and believed that the evacuation of Fort Sumter would indicate his recognition of the Confederacy. He also knew that attempts to strengthen the troops by force might lead to the secession of Virginia and other loyal states.

Lincoln decided to supply the fort peaceably. He contacted South Carolina authorities, ignoring the Confederate government, and explained that no force would be used to complete the mission.

The Confederacy needed the Charleston harbor. Knowing that supply boats would not be able to sail past Fort Sumter if it were held by federal troops, the Confederate States called for the surrender of Fort Sumter before Lincoln's supply ships could arrive. They would have no need to fire on a peaceful expedition, and they could also retain the prestige they had earned as defenders of their property against aggression.

When Major Anderson received the Confederate message, he decided not to evacuate but to hold the fort until he could hear from Lincoln. On the morning of April 12, 1861, before any news could reach Anderson, General P.G.T. Beauregard ordered the bombardment of Fort Sumter. The shore batteries continued until Anderson lowered the American flag thirty-four hours later when the Union troops had used all of their ammunition and food stores.

On April 15, Lincoln declared the Southern insurrection was "too powerful to be suppressed by the ordinary course of judicial proceedings." Lincoln called for seventy-five thousand volunteers to enlist in the military service for three months and ordered the navy to blockade all the ports of the South.

Lincoln's call for troops led Virginia to vote for secession, joining the seven Southern commonwealths already in the Confederacy. The consequent secession of Arkansas, North Carolina, and Tennessee placed all but four of the slave states in the Confederacy. Maryland, Kentucky, Missouri, and Delaware remained in the Union as border states.

Three of these states rejected Lincoln's call for federal troops and declared individual "armed neutrality." Lincoln immediately took steps to keep these state governments from arming the people against the Union. He sent in federal troops to occupy Maryland, supplied Union sympathizers with arms in Kentucky, approved of a new pro-Union state government in Missouri and ousted the pro-Confederate officials in office. Only Delaware was spared federal intervention to retain her "loyalty."

Every state of the Confederacy except South Carolina contained counties that were pro-Union and that voted to remain loyal. The loyal counties in western Virginia banded together and seceded from the new Confederate state, entering the Union in as West Virginia in 1863.

Robert E. Lee

Robert E. Lee, a Virginian, was torn between loyalty to the Union and loyalty to his state. Even though he owned no slaves and opposed secession, his love for Virginia was strong. Ultimately, he joined the Southern army, and the Confederacy gained its greatest general. During the Civil War, men from the South who believed in the Union fought on the Northern side and Confederate sympathizers from the North wore the gray uniform of the South. Tragically, brothers fought brothers and fathers fought sons across the Mason-Dixon line.

A major contention of the Confederacy was the insistence on the preeminence of states' rights over the central government. This belief led to quarrels between state officials and Confederate officials and between officeholders in the capital. Jefferson Davis was never able to forge a united Confederacy of the commonwealth states. He was unable to raise an army of men from all over the South because each state insisted on keeping its own troops. Alexander H. Stephens, his vice president, opposed most of Davis' plans and accused Davis of disregarding the rights of the states.

Fill in the blanks.

2.1   The vocabulary word meaning *metal money* is _____ .

2.2   Abraham Lincoln was the candidate for the _____ party.

2.3   The candidate for the Southern Democratic party was _____ of Kentucky.

2.4   The Northern Democrats nominated _____ as their presidential candidate.

2.5   _____ was elected president of the Confederacy.

2.6   _____ was elected vice president of the Confederacy.

2.7   Four states that seceded after the fall of Fort Sumter were _____ , _____ , _____ , and _____ .

2.8   The greatest general in the Southern army was _____ .

2.9   President Buchanan said that secession was unconstitutional, but the government had no power _____ against a state.

True/False.

2.10   _____   John Bell's Constitutional Union Party favored preservation of the Union and denounced slavery.

2.11   _____   The Southern Democrats refused to nominate Stephen Douglas because he would not change his stand on popular sovereignty.

2.12   _____   The Republican platform approved the protective tariff, supported the extension of slavery into the territories, and supported federal funding for internal improvements.

2.13   _____   President Lincoln urged the South to reconsider its actions before seceding.

2.14   _____   The commander at Fort Sumter was Major Robert Anderson.

2.15   _____   Lincoln did not want to send more troops to Fort Sumter because of the possible secession of Virginia and other loyal states.

2.16   _____   The Confederacy needed control of Fort Sumter, located in Charleston harbor.

2.17   _____   The battle for Fort Sumter began on April 12, 1861.

2.18   _____   President Lincoln replaced Major Anderson with General P.G.T. Beauregard.

2.19   _____   After thirty-four hours of continual fighting, Fort Sumter fell to the South.

Choose the best answer(s).

2.20   What percent of the popular vote did Lincoln receive in the 1860 presidential election?

_____   a. more than 40%

_____   b. less than 40%

_____   c. 40%

_____   d. 48%

2.21   Who were Lincoln's three opponents in the 1860 presidential race?

_____   a. John Bell

_____   b. Salmon Chase

_____   c. William Seward

_____   d. Stephen Douglas

_____   e. John Breckinridge

_____   f. Sam Houston

2.22   Which state was first to secede from the Union?

_____   a. Mississippi

_____   b. Georgia

_____   c. North Carolina

_____   d. South Carolina

2.23   Which six states immediately followed the first state in secession?

_____   a. Missouri

_____   b. Mississippi

_____   c. Tennessee

_____   d. Georgia

_____   e. Kentucky

_____   f. Louisiana

_____   g. Florida

_____   h. North Carolina

_____   i. South Carolina

_____   j. Texas

_____   k. Alabama

HISTORY & GEOGRAPHY

1 1 0 5

LIFEPAC TEST

66/83

Name _____

Date _____

Score _____

HISTORY AND GEOGRAPHY 1105 LIFEPAC TEST

True/False (each answer, 1 point)

1. _____ The South had better military leaders than the North.

2. _____ The North had more manpower than the South.

3. _____ The slave state with more free black people than slaves was Virginia.

4. _____ Agriculture was the leading occupation in the United States during the mid-1800s.

5. _____ Slavery held the South in bondage to an archaic way of life.

6. _____ The black codes placed restrictions on black people.

7. _____ The North was the most rural and agrarian of all the regions in the United States.

8. _____ The Freedman's Bureau was created to help black persons adjust to their new freedom and to tell them how to vote.

9. _____ The destruction of the "Southern way of life" was not caused by the loss of slaves, but by the loss of capital and destruction of property during the Civil War

10. _____ Manifest Destiny was the idea that Americans had the right to all the land from the Atlantic Ocean to the Pacific Ocean.

11. _____ Fredericksburg was a Union victory.

12. _____ Rice was the leading crop raised in the South.

13. _____ William T. Sherman cut a path of destruction across Georgia on his march to the sea.

14. _____ John Bell of the Constitutional Union party ran for the presidency against Lincoln on a strong antislavery platform.

15. _____ The Great Plains was the best region for agriculture before the Civil War.

16. _____ The labor supply in New England was suitable for textile manufacturing.

17. _____ The Confederacy adopted the "Stars and Stripes" as its national flag.

Match these places and descriptions (each answer, 2 points).

18. _____ Cincinnati   a. most populous Western state

19. _____ Chicago   b. Lincoln assassinated

20 _____ Richmond   c. taken by Farragut

21. _____ Fort Sumter   d. pork-packing center

22. _____ South Carolina   e. first state to secede

23. _____ Appomattox Court House   f. first battle of Civil War

24. _____ Gettysburg   g. site of surrender

25. _____ Ford Theater   h. turning point of Civil War

26. _____ New Orleans   i. railroad capital

27. _____ Ohio   j. Confederate capital

Match these men with their descriptions (each answer, 2 points).

28. _____ Major Robert Anderson   a. president of the Confederacy

29. _____ James Buchanan   b. "No terms except immediate and unconditional surrender"

30. _____ Abraham Lincoln   c. Lincoln's vice president

31. _____ Edwin M. Stanton   d. invented the telegraph

32. _____ Samuel F. B. Morse   e. president when the Reconstruction ended

33. _____ Rutherford B. Hayes   f. president during Civil War

34. _____ General Winfield Scott   g. commander of Fort Sumter

35. _____ Andrew Johnson   h. proponent of the "divide and conquer" plan to win the Civil War

36. _____ Ulysses S. Grant   i. secretary of war removed by Johnson

37. _____ Jefferson Davis   j. president when South Carolina seceded

Match these laws and acts with their descriptions (each answer, 2 points).

38. _____ Thirteenth Amendment

39. _____ Fourteenth Amendment

40. _____ Wade-Davis Bill

41. _____ Black Codes

42. _____ Tenure of Office Act

43. _____ Reconstruction Act

44. _____ Command of the Army Act

45. _____ Ku Klux Klan Act

46. _____ Amnesty Act

47. _____ grandfather clause

a. divided South into five military districts

b. former Confederates became eligible to vote

c. abolished slavery

d. gave black people citizenship

e. exempted white voters from literacy test

f. put restrictions on black people

g. an effort to end the activities of a secret, anti-black society

h. president could not remove federal officials from office

i. required oath of majority before readmission

j. could not issue presidential orders directly to the army

Fill in the blanks (each answer, 3 points).

48. The commander of the Union army at the end of the Civil War was

_____ .

49. The commander of the Confederate army at the end of the Civil War was

_____ .

THE ANTAGONISTS

After the fall of Fort Sumter, both North and South began preparing for the inevitable confrontations. Activity behind the Union and Confederate lines in search of men was extremely active. Although the North held most of the advantages in resources, the South had the best qualified leaders and the advantage of fighting on their own soil.

Northern preparations. After the fall of Fort Sumter, thousands of men answered Lincoln's call for volunteers. Such enthusiasm did not last, however, and federal, state, and local governments had to offer bounties to encourage volunteers to sign up for military service. In 1863, two years after the war began, the North resorted to conscription but allowed drafted men to pay three hundred dollars in lieu of service. Poor people resisted this inequity and staged riots in some of the North's larger cities.

The money necessary for warfare was raised by passing the Morrill Tariff, with duties increased to the 1846 levels. The tariff also protected Northern manufacturers from foreign competition and helped to increase production.

Paper money called "greenbacks" was issued in 1862 after the excise tax and the income tax, initiated earlier, had not generated sufficient funds. The value of the greenbacks, which were circulated as regular money, would vary depending upon the ability of the federal government to redeem them. As the fortunes of the Union rose and fell, so did the value of the greenbacks. The North also sold war bonds to individuals and to banks and passed the National Banking Act, which required nationally chartered banks to purchase government bonds.

With troops and financing secured, the North began developing a strategy for winning the war. First, the blockade would continue, with no ships allowed to enter or leave Southern ports to prevent the exportation of cotton and the importation of munitions from foreign nations. Second, the Confederacy was to be divided in half by capturing key transportation centers along the Mississippi and thereby gaining control of the river. Third, the eastern portion of the Confederacy was to be split by sending troops from the Mississippi across to Atlanta and on to the Atlantic coast. Finally, the Confederate capital, Richmond, Virginia, was to be captured. Soldiers would then march from Richmond to meet Union troops returning from the Mississippi campaigns.

Northern advantages. A comparison of the North and South reveals that all the material factors were on the side of the North. These advantages became more important as the war continued.

The North had six major advantages:

1. More than two-thirds of the people in the United States lived in the North, 22 million people against 9.5 million in the South, with more than 3 million of the Southerners being unarmed slaves. This difference in population meant that the North had more available manpower for military duty without depleting the factories and farms.

2. Manufacturing interests were centered in the North. More than 90 percent of the nation's industries and three-fourths of the nation's capital were held by this region.

3. Natural resources necessary to supply the factories or to trade with other countries were also available in the North. Iron, coal, copper, gold, and other metals and minerals important to the war cause were available to the Union, but not to the Confederacy.

4. Agricultural products were available from the western part of the Union. The North was able to feed its troops and to trade valuable wheat to European countries.

5. Transportation of men, equipment, and supplies was easily accomplished on the twenty thousand miles of Northern railroad lines.

6. Plans were developed through an established government and implemented by an established army and navy.

As the war lengthened, the advantages of the North became more important. The ability to provide adequate food, clothing, and shoes for the troops was easier in the North where agriculture was diversified and factories produced massive amounts of war supplies. In the South, where imports were practically cut off, the people had to do without many products. The factories were not able to obtain adequate raw materials. Moreover, the small number of men left on the farms meant that women and children had to grow the food for themselves and for the soldiers.

Southern preparations. Volunteers joined the Confederate army in each state as it seceded from the Union but when more men were needed, the South was forced to resort to conscription. Southern conscription was not successful; the intense states' rights attitude of the people kept them from totally cooperating with the new central government. Each commonwealth set occupational exemptions on the draft, and men could buy a substitute to serve their three-year term. Like the poor in the North, the Southerners resented what appeared to be "a rich man's war and a poor man's fight."

Financing the war was more difficult in the South than in the North because most of the region's wealth was tied up in slaves and other property. The Confederacy levied an excise tax, sold bonds to individuals, and issued paper money to help fill the treasury. The Confederate money did not have a **specie** backing and declined in value as the prospects for a Southern victory dimmed. The South attempted to borrow money from European banks but was unsuccessful.

Southern advantages. Although financially poor and low in population, the South had some decisive advantages over the North in the upcoming conflict.

1. The South had only to hold its territory and to fight a defensive war. They planned to repel the Northern intruders at every point until they tired of battle and decided to recognize the Confederacy as a separate country. The Confederacy planned on aggressive action, however. It planned to divide the industrial Northeast from the Midwest, charging north into Maryland and Pennsylvania.

2. Southerners were relatively united by their belief in the necessity and honor of fighting for their way of life. They were accustomed to hunting and riding; consequently, all classes of Southern men were more prepared for the rigors of battle than were the Northern city dwellers. Southerners were also familiar with the terrain and climate of their home states.

3. Many of the nation's trained and experienced army officers were West Point graduates from the South. Almost all of these men resigned their commissions and joined the Confederate army. Thomas "Stonewall" Jackson and Robert E. Lee were both West Point graduates who fought diligently for the Southern cause.

The South expected "King Cotton" to be an advantage. Southern leaders thought that people in Britain and France who favored the Southern aristocracy and wanted the tariff on their manufactured goods dropped would encourage their government to support the South. Southerners were sure that the need for cotton would guarantee aid from these countries. Diplomatic maneuvers by the North in the Trent Affair, however, restricted Britain's involvement to building ships like the *Alabama* while France remained neutral.

Complete this chart to show the advantages held by each side at the beginning of the Civil War. If the advantage was held by the North, mark the box in the North column; if it was held by the South, mark the box in that column.

	Advantages	North	South
2.24	A larger source of manpower	☐	☐
2.25	Established governmental agencies	☐	☐
2.26	Troops physically prepared for fighting	☐	☐
2.27	Available natural resources	☐	☐
2.28	A defensive stand	☐	☐
2.29	Familiar with terrain and climate	☐	☐
2.30	Adequate transportation	☐	☐
2.31	Superior military leadership	☐	☐
2.32	Diversified agriculture	☐	☐
2.33	Factories able to produce munitions and supplies	☐	☐

Choose the best answer(s).

2.34   The border slave states included:

_____   a. Maryland

_____   b. Pennsylvania

_____   c. Kansas

_____   d. Kentucky

_____   e. Missouri

_____   f. Delaware

_____   g. Virginia

Fill in the blanks.

2.35   Many Southern army officers were graduates of _____ .

2.36   Southerners were sure that the need for _____ would gain the support of the

countries of _____ and _____ .

2.37   The Northern strategists wanted to capture the Confederate capital of _____

in _____ .

Match these items with the best description.

2.38   _____   the *Alabama*   a. raised money for the North

2.39   _____   P.G.T. Beauregard   b. commanded Confederate forces

2.40   _____   Morrill Tariff   c. came from Britain

2.41   _____   greenbacks   d. ordered the bombardment of Fort Sumter

2.42   _____   "Stonewall" Jackson   e. issued as Northern currency

CIVIL WAR: UNION BLOCKADE AND HOSTILITIES

The abundant natural and manufactured resources of the North gave it a definite military advantage over the South. The North capitalized on this advantage by instituting a naval blockade of all Southern ports, thus cutting off the flow of supplies to and from the South.

THE UNION BLOCKADE

In April 1861, while calling for volunteers to serve their country, President Lincoln ordered the Union blockade of Southern ports. The Union blockade was one of the most effective installations of the war. Two hundred sixty-four armed Union ships patrolled the three hundred miles of the Atlantic and Gulf coasts from Virginia to Texas. The blockade effectively stopped ships trying to enter or leave Southern ports and Southerners began to feel the result when store shelves became bare.

Guns and ammunition could not be imported and, because the South had only a few factories, they were not able to make enough ammunition to keep up with the demand. The few railroads the South had were in need of repair, limiting their usefulness for transporting men and supplies.

Adequate medicine and hospital equipment were not available and limited quantities of salt meant that fresh meat could not be preserved for the soldiers. Tea, coffee, flour, soap, matches, needles, and other manufactured or processed goods were in short supply. Cotton, the source of cash for most Southerners, could not be exported across the blockade.

Occasionally sleek, low-lying ships that were painted dark colors to reduce their visibility penetrated the blockade and brought supplies to the South. However, the blockade all but eliminated these inroads before the end of the war. In one instance a Confederate boat was confiscated and sailed past Fort Sumter into the Union lines. This daring act brought former slave, Robert Smalls, into the Union ranks. Smalls served as pilot and captain of the ship that was to later be engaged in several naval battles.

The most famous naval battle occurred when the Confederate ironclad ship, the *Merrimac* (later renamed the *Virginia*) attacked Union ships in Hampton Roads before McClellan's peninsular campaign. Hoping to break the Union blockade, the South was disappointed when the *Merrimac* was met by the *Monitor*, a new Union ironclad with a specially-designed revolving gun turret. During the battle, neither ship was able to damage the other effectively. It was the first naval battle in history between metal plated ships. This battle marked the beginning of a new era in naval warfare, but the South was unable to break the blockade.

35

Merrimac vs. *Monitor*

THE HOSTILITIES

By the summer of 1861, both sides were prepared for the hostilities. The South had fallen heir to well-stocked federal arsenals and was convinced they could defend their cause of independence. The North's material advantage was not in evidence at this time, but they were committed to quelling the rebellion and restoring the Union.

The strategies. General Winfield Scott, a Southerner who remained loyal to the concept of the Union, was the Union Army General-in-Chief. General Scott had served in the War of 1812 and the Mexican War and was prepared to serve his country again. Scott was 65 years old but a clear thinker; he was the one person most responsible for the Union's blockade of Southern ports and the "divide and conquer" plan that was initially rejected by the other officers in the army. General Scott proposed that the Union forces capture the Mississippi River and then separate the lower South from the upper South through land campaigns. Northern military leaders rejected the plan because they feared the Confederates would try to capture Washington, D.C.

In the South, Jefferson Davis continued to believe that the North would allow the South to secede without "war." He wanted to take a defensive stance that would show the world that the South wanted only to separate from the Union, not conquer it. Davis was unable to persuade his generals that the defensive plan was best for the South. Some believed that a Confederate offensive displaying the superior skills of Southern soldiers would help keep the war as short as possible. It is also probable that some farsighted generals realized that a long war would eventually spell the end of the Confederacy.

General Winfield Scott

Northern strategists prepared to capture the Confederate capital, Richmond, Virginia, about one hundred miles from Washington, D.C. Northern generals supposed that the capture of its capital would collapse the Confederacy.

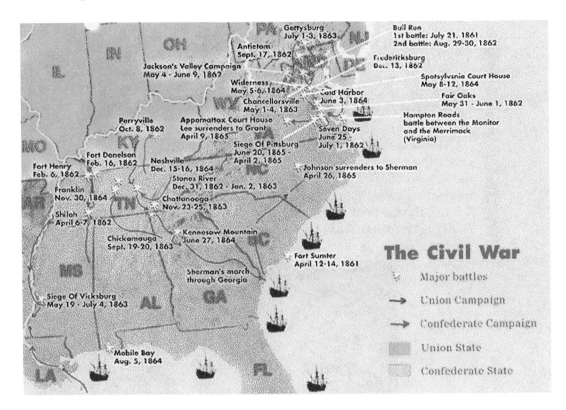

The engagement. On both sides of the dividing line, generals and volunteers prepared to meet each other in the first major battle of the war. General Irvin McDowell marched south with thirty thousand men to Manassas, a railroad junction in Virginia and the approach to Richmond. Twenty-four thousand Confederate troops under the command of P.G.T. Beauregard and "Stonewall" Jackson met the Yankees in the First Battle of Bull Run. Men and women from Washington followed in the wake of the Union soldiers with picnic baskets to watch the defeat of the South. The inexperienced Union soldiers were disorganized. The similarity of the uniforms and flags contributed to the confusion that led to the death of about forty-five hundred soldiers.

During the day, as the fight raged on, a Union victory seemed imminent. The Confederate troops seemed beaten when General Thomas J. Jackson took his famed "stonewall" stand and held one section of the field while the Rebels, reinforced by General Joseph E. Johnston, drove the Union troops from the battlefield with their fury and courage. The retreat toward Washington included an unknown infantryman, William T. Sherman and a young cavalryman, George Armstrong Custer.

William T. Sherman

George Armstrong Custer

Rushing out of the way, the spectators certainly had seen more than they expected. The defeat of "their side" was shattering, and most had never envisioned the tragedy of war in terms of the human suffering they saw that day. No more battlefield picnics occurred after Bull Run.

Flushed with victory, the South became more confident of quickly winning the war. Defeat helped the Union to recognize the conflict would not be so easy as supposed nor would it be as short as expected.

Lincoln removed the defeated General McDowell from command of the army and appointed General George B. McClellan in his place as commander of the eastern campaign. McClellan, an ambitious young man of thirty-four, gladly accepted his assignment and eventually replaced Winfield Scott as Lincoln's General-in-Chief.

General McClellan was well known for his ability to organize and condition troops. He spent the next nine months doing just that. His trained troops did not leave Washington until April of 1862, three months after Lincoln issued General War Order No. 1, in which he declared Washington's birthday, February 22, as a day of general movement of the United States land and naval forces. During this period of quiet on the Potomac while General McClellan was training his troops in combat skills, the western Confederate troops were meeting defeat at the hands of Union officers.

General McDowell   General McClellan

Western campaign. Fort Henry on the Tennessee River and Fort Donelson on the Cumberland River were important Confederate strongholds against Union control of the Mississippi River. These forts protected Confederate lines of communication along the network of rivers feeding into the Ohio and the Mississippi. The railroads connecting the eastern section of the South with the West, where many of the raw products necessary to the existence of the Confederate army were produced, terminated at Memphis and Vicksburg, just beyond Fort Donelson and Fort Henry. Union forces were anxious to capture these forts. The Union army hoped not only to deprive the Southern forces of products from the Southwest but also to deflate the morale of the Confederacy which was still elated by early victories in the East.

General John Pope, General George H. Thomas, Commodore Andrew H. Foote, and General Ulysses S. Grant won a number of battles that brought the Union troops to the gates of the twin forts. At Fort Donelson, Grant issued the ultimatum that helped him become a national hero, "No terms except immediate and unconditional surrender."

The Confederate General of the forces at Fort Donelson, General Albert Johnston, pulled back to Corinth, Mississippi, a strategic railroad center. The circumstance that gave General Johnston sufficient time to rebuild his forces and to fortify their position was Grant's inability to pursue his objective. Grant was relieved of duty and his troops dispersed to other generals for tactical movement at this crucial time. When Grant resumed command of his troops, he followed the orders of his commander, General Halleck and pressed forward toward Pittsburgh Landing on the Tennessee River. Grant had orders to wait there for reinforcements from General Buell.

Before Buell could reach Grant's camp, Johnston attacked the Union troops near the Shiloh church. During the first day of furious fighting, it seemed that Grant's forces would be defeated by this surprise attack at the Battle of Shiloh. The death of their general, however, weakened the resolve of the Rebels; and the appearance of Buell's forces helped Grant to repel the Confederate attack.

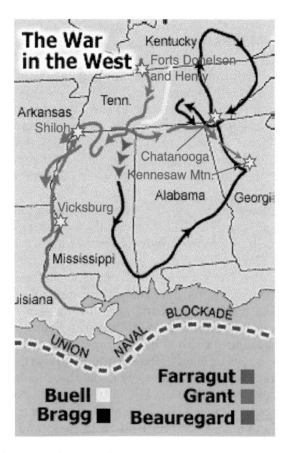

After the battle, thirteen thousand Union casualties and ten thousand Confederate casualties lay in the fields. The human loss led to severe criticism of Grant and the insistence by some that Grant be removed from command. Lincoln, impressed with Grant's fighting, insisted that he remain in command. When Halleck was appointed commander of the Union armies in the East, Grant succeeded to Halleck's command in the West.

In the month after Shiloh, the Union forces pressed toward Corinth, Mississippi, a railroad center between Memphis and Chattanooga, Tennessee. By June the Union forces had gained control of the Mississippi as far as Memphis.

In Richmond the Confederate officials watched the retreat down the Mississippi with dismay. General Robert E. Lee, a presidential advisor to Jefferson Davis, warned that the lower Mississippi was all-important to the existence of the Confederacy. Robert E. Lee, a moral man and splendid soldier, was a member of one of the leading families in Virginia. He, like many other Southern generals, had been an officer in the United States army until the secession of his home state. Then the ties of family and home swayed his concern more toward those of his state and of his nation. Lee did not own any slaves when the war began—he had indeed inherited a number. Believing slavery had an evil effect on the owners and the slaves, Lee had freed those slaves in bondage to him long before the war.

Robert E. Lee

Southern loyalty caused Lee to resign his commission and to sever his friendship with General Scott, his commanding officer and close friend. Lee wrote to his sister: "...I hope I may never be called upon to draw my sword." The circumstances of war determined otherwise, however, and Lee became the commander of the Confederate army.

Soon after Shiloh, Captain David G. Farragut led a Union fleet through Confederate lines at the mouth of the Mississippi and into the port New Orleans. The Union troops commanded by Benjamin F. Butler followed Farragut into New Orleans and occupied the city on May 1, 1862. Other federal troops left New Orleans and sailed up the Mississippi toward Memphis until only Vicksburg, Mississippi, and Port Hudson, Louisiana restricted complete Union control of the mighty river.

Eastern campaign. On the east coast after the bitter cold of winter rain and snow was over, "Little Mac," General McClellan moved his forces to Fort Monroe on the Virginia peninsula and planned to march to the Confederate capital of Richmond. Relying on information about Confederate troops he received from Allan Pinkerton, the head of a detective agency, McClellan was overly cautious and failed to attack the city. Before the Union troops reached the capital, they were met and repelled by General Johnston in the battle of Seven Pines. Johnston sustained an injury and the brilliant Robert E. Lee assumed his command.

McClellan's plans for the army of the Potomac depended on reinforcements from Washington. The Washington generals, however, were busy protecting the Union capital from the dashing forays of General "Stonewall" Jackson, who approached Washington, D.C. across the Shenandoah Valley and resisted several attempts by Union troops to capture his forces. His objective accomplished, Jackson returned to the peninsula, leaving a large number of Union troops guarding the capital instead of joining forces with General McClellan.

Lee, now commander of the army of northern Virginia, sent his scout, Jeb Stuart, to gather information on the position of the federal troops. Stuart was seen by the Union troops and, being warned of impending attack, they prepared for battle. Lee met the Union soldiers in the Seven Days' Battle. Although the attack was not a surprise as Lee had planned and the Confederate loss was as great as the Union loss, the army of the Potomac retreated to the James River where the Union troops could be evacuated.

Disturbed by the performance of McClellan's troops, Lincoln relieved the general of his command and placed General Halleck in command of the eastern forces, leaving McClellan in charge of the army of the Potomac. Halleck named John Pope, one of his generals from the victorious West, to lead the land forces marching toward Richmond and ordered McClellan to join forces with Pope. Lee, seeing an opportunity to attack this much smaller army under Pope's command before McClellan could sail up the Potomac, joined forces with "Stonewall" Jackson and defeated Pope in the second battle of Bull Run.

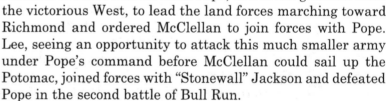
National Archives   John Pope

Lee, flushed with victory, pressed toward the Harper's Ferry arsenal near the border of Maryland where he planned to secure munitions and supplies for the Confederate troops as well as gain new recruits from Confederate sympathizers. Motivated by the belief that another Confederate victory would swell the antiwar chorus in the North and secure European intervention, Lee marched toward Union territory.

Lee's troops were near Sharpsburg, Maryland on the Antietam Creek when McClellan and his troops attacked. Lee's forty thousand men resisted the Union attack five times, but ten thousand Confederate soldiers paid with their lives. Twelve thousand Union men died, and Antietam became known as the bloodiest one-day battle in the war. The apprehensive McClellan did not follow through and lost the chance of a decisive victory when he let Lee slip away under the cloak of night during a lull in the fighting.

Fill in the blanks.

2.43   The Union naval blockade involved _____ ships over a _____ -mile stretch of sea.

2.44   The black slave who would later captain a Union ship was _____ _____ .

2.45   The most famous naval battle of the war was between the _____
and the _____ .

2.46   The battle of the *Merrimac* and the *Monitor* was the beginning of a new era in naval warfare
because _____ .

2.47   Cutting the Confederacy from east and west and north and south was General Scott's strategy
of _____ .

2.48   The commander-in-chief of the Confederate Army was _____ .

2.49   The port of New Orleans was taken by _____ while
_____ occupied the city on May 1, 1862.

Match these people and battles to their proper descriptions.

2.50   _____ Battle of Seven Pines   a. commanded Union forces in the East

2.51   _____ George B. McClellan   b. Johnston and Lee attacked McClellan

2.52   _____ "Stonewall" Jackson   c. defeated Pope in the second battle of Bull Run

2.53   _____ Robert E. Lee   d. bloodiest single-day battle

2.54   _____ General Halleck   e. kept Union army in Washington, D.C.

2.55   _____ Jackson and Lee   f. commanded army of Virginia

2.56   _____ Antietam   g. commanded army of the Potomac

2.57   After his defeat at Bull Run General McDowell was replaced by General:

    _____ a. Custer.

    _____ b. McClellan.

    _____ c. Grant.

    _____ d. Jackson.

2.58   General War Order No. 1 was an order for Union forces to move against the South on:

    _____ a. February 12.

    _____ b. April 16.

    _____ c. February 22.

    _____ d. April 10.

2.59   Fort Henry was located on the:

    _____ a. Tennessee River.

    _____ b. Ohio River.

    _____ c. Kentucky River.

    _____ d. Mississippi River.

2.60   Fort Donelson was taken by General:

    _____ a. Grant.

    _____ b. Pope.

    _____ c. Jackson.

    _____ d. Lee.

2.61   General Grant defeated the Confederate forces at Pittsburgh Landing in the battle of:

    _____ a. Nashville.

    _____ b. Vicksburg.

    _____ c. Gettysburg.

    _____ d. Shiloh.

2.62   Who warned Jefferson Davis that the lower Mississippi was important to the existence of the Confederacy?

    _____ a. Grant

    _____ b. Jackson

    _____ c. Lee

    _____ d. Butler

THE CIVIL WAR: FINAL PHASE

When the war was approaching its third year, President Lincoln issued his Emancipation Proclamation, setting the slaves free in all states still in rebellion against the United States. Freed slaves formed two regiments for the Union and were instrumental in ensuing battles.

The hostilities reached their high point in the greatest battle of the war, Gettysburg. From this battle the struggle continued for almost two more years, ending with the terms Grant gave to Lee at Appomattox Court House on April 9, 1865.

The strategy of slavery. Whenever Union troops were victorious in the South, black people working on Confederate fortifications and entrenchments or laboring in the fields of nearby plantations would flee to the Union lines. The Union soldiers, without directives from the federal government, acted according to their own beliefs and principles. As a result, slaves were repelled and sent South; some were held as contraband or as prisoners. Others were impressed into domestic service for the officers and troops. Many donned the uniform of the Union army and fought valiantly for the freedom of their brothers.

Although the question of slavery seemed to many to be at the forefront of the causes for the Civil War, Lincoln was emphatic in his denial of this assertion. He believed that the preservation of the Union, at all costs, was of supreme importance and that this reason was the chief motive for fighting the war.

Under pressure from antislavery forces, Lincoln signed a bill abolishing slavery in Washington, D.C. in April, 1862 and another bill in June abolishing slavery in the territories. Lincoln eventually saw that the end of slavery might be a method of preserving the Union. He decided to wait for a Union victory before making an announcement. After Antietam when Lee fled Northern ground, Lincoln issued the preliminary Emancipation Proclamation, declaring that all slaves in the rebelling states would be free on January 1, 1863. He hoped to draw some Rebels back to the Union by including a passage that offered compensation to those owners not in rebellion on January 1, 1863 and who adopted immediate or gradual abolishment of slavery. Lincoln promised to relocate those blacks who wished to leave the United States and he emphasized that no federal assistance would be given to slave owners if their slaves rebelled or ran away. However, the Emancipation Proclamation claiming that slaves "henceforward shall be free" did not set one slave free, nor did it shorten the war as Lincoln had hoped. It was, however, the beginning of the end for slavery in America.

Gen. Ambrose E. Burnside   Gen. Robert E. Lee

Generals At Fredericksburg

Fredericksburg. In December of 1862, Lee met General Ambrose E. Burnside, the newest of Lincoln's appointments, in Fredericksburg on the banks of the Rappahannock River. In a foolhardy attempt, General Burnside tried to take Lee's forces, which were fortified at the top of a series of hills. The Union lost more than twelve thousand men during the confrontation. Burnside retreated with his remaining troops and asked to be relieved of his command.

Burnside was replaced by General Joseph E. Hooker who met Lee in battle and was defeated at Chancellorsville. The Union troops again retreated. Lee seemed to have the Union troops on the run, but misfortune claimed the life of his finest General, "Stonewall" Jackson. As he returned to his camp after dark, Jackson was mortally wounded by one of his own men who thought he was a Union scout.

Gen. Joseph E. Hooker

Gen. "Stonewall" Jackson

Gen. George Meade

Gettysburg. The victorious but saddened Lee once again decided to cross the Union line. He marched with seventy thousand men across Maryland toward Harrisburg, Pennsylvania and reached the farthest Northern point of Confederate penetration. There he met General George Meade near the little town of Gettysburg.

The battle lasted three days, ending with the defeat of General Lee. He gathered his remaining troops and retreated toward Richmond. In the fields of Gettysburg lay almost forty-six thousand men dead or wounded. Four months after this turning point in the war, President Lincoln traveled to Gettysburg for the dedication of a cemetery at the battle site. Here Lincoln gave his famous Gettysburg Address.

Vicksburg. On July 4, 1863, the day after the Union victory at Gettysburg, Lincoln heard of the Union triumphs in the West. Vicksburg, Mississippi had been the only serious stronghold against Union command of the mighty river. The navy had bombarded the city from the river, and Grant had tried to capture the city by land five times. Grant marched

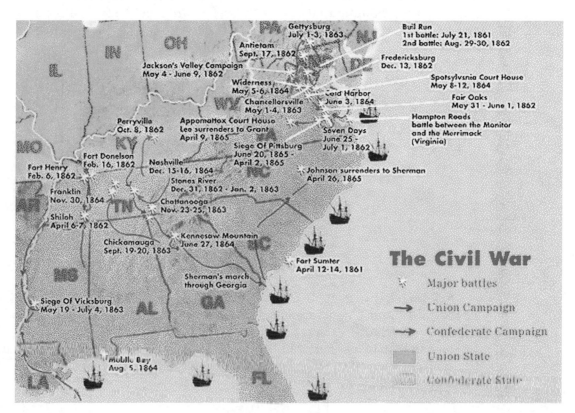

his troops down the west side of the Mississippi and waited downstream for Rear Admiral David D. Porter to run the fleet of gunboats and transports past the Vicksburg batteries. He would then carry the Union troops across to the east shore where the men could march north and capture the city. Vicksburg was well protected and repulsed the attack. Grant, however, cut the city's access to supplies and communications with other Confederate troops, and forty-seven days later on July 4, Vicksburg surrendered. Union control of the Mississippi effectively cut the Confederate communications to the trans-Mississippi Rebel states and kept supplies from these states from reaching the battle-weary soldiers.

Important Civil War Sites

Chickamauga. The next Union target in the South was Chattanooga, an important railroad terminal. Union and Confederate troops met at Chickamauga Creek, where the Union troops were defeated and were forced to retreat to Chattanooga. The Confederates held them in the city until, cut off from supplies, the men were close to starvation. The Union troops did not surrender but held out for reinforcements. They were rescued when troops under the leadership of Grant routed the Confederates and chased them into Georgia. These forces were composed of troops traveling by rail across the states from the army of the Potomac and those led by William Sherman, traveling on foot from Vicksburg. After Chattanooga, General Grant was appointed to the highest office in the army; he accepted the post of lieutenant-general in the spring of 1864.

Sherman's campaign. The capture of Chattanooga gave the infamous General William T. Sherman a base for his devastating march to the sea. He began by working his way south to Atlanta, Georgia, which he captured in August.

Grant, in the meantime, traveled east and took personal command of the army of the Potomac. The aggressive Grant chased Lee into the South and met him in a series of indecisive battles at the Wilderness and Cold Harbor. Grant lost some fifty-five thousand men in the first month. Then, despairing of capturing Lee, Grant decided to try capturing Richmond. In June of 1864, Grant moved his troops toward Petersburg, twenty miles south of Richmond. At Petersburg, Confederate troops moved to block Grant's advance. The

Union troops dug trenches around Petersburg and held the Confederates inside the city for nine months but were not able to penetrate their lines.

Lincoln's four years in office were running out and the war still raged. In spite of this fact, Lincoln was nominated for a second term and ran on the Republican ticket with Andrew Johnson. His opponent was the Northern Democratic candidate, General George McClellan, the reluctant fighter from the eastern campaigns.

Sherman's stunning victory in Atlanta secured the election for Lincoln. Lincoln won 212 electoral votes of all the Union states except Kentucky, Delaware, and New Jersey and received about 55 percent of the popular vote. In his second inaugural address he implored the people of the nation to work for the cessation of the war.

When Sherman left Atlanta, his purpose was to separate the lower South from the rest of the Confederacy. His troops burned and killed everything in their path in their march across Georgia from Atlanta to Savannah. He reached Savannah in December and left in his wake a trail of devastation sixty miles wide and three hundred miles long. In February of 1865, representatives of the two opposing governments met at Hampton Roads, Virginia for peace talks. Lincoln's conditions did not waver—reunion of the states and emancipation of the slaves. He proposed a limited compensation to slave holders for their losses, but Davis refused anything but Southern independence.

Sherman then turned toward Richmond. The Confederate troops could see the jaws of the Union closing as Grant in the North and Sherman in the South marched toward each other. When Grant captured Lee's supply lines to Richmond, the Confederate troops evacuated Petersburg. In April of 1865, faced by overwhelming odds, Lee evacuated Richmond sometime after Jefferson Davis had fled to Montgomery, Alabama. Lee hoped to march to North Carolina and join forces with other Confederate holdouts, but the Union forces had cut off all lines of retreat.

Lee and Grant met at Appomattox Court House, west of Richmond, on April 9, 1865. There, the tired and saddened General Lee signed the surrender that ended the war. Grant, following Lincoln's orders, allowed the troops to keep their horses and provided food for the hungry, striving to carry out the sentiments in Lincoln's second inaugural address:

> "With malice toward none; with charity for all; with firmness In the right as God gives us to see the right, let us strive on to finish the work we are in; to bind up the nation's wounds; to care for him who shall have borne the battle and for his widow and his orphan— to do all which may achieve and cherish a just and lasting peace among ourselves and with all nations."

True/False.

2.63 _____ After Union victories in the South, blacks would cross over to the Union lines.

2.64 _____ Many of the blacks fought for the North in the latter part of the war.

2.65 _____ Lincoln's Emancipation Proclamation set all the slaves free.

2.66 _____ Lincoln promised to compensate those slave owners who were not in rebellion as of January 1, 1863.

2.67 _____ The Emancipation Proclamation brought a quick end to the war.

2.68 _____ General Burnside defeated General Lee at Fredericksburg.

2.69 _____ General Hooker was defeated by Lee at Chancellorsville.

2.70 _____ The turning point of the Civil War was the Battle of Gettysburg.

2.71 _____ General Lee was defeated at Gettysburg and "Stonewall" Jackson was killed.

2.72 _____ More than seventy thousand men were killed or wounded at Gettysburg.

Fill in the blanks.

2.73 General Grant and Admiral Porter tried five times to capture _____ _____ before succeeding.

2.74 Vicksburg surrendered on _____ .

2.75 With the capture of Vicksburg, all Confederate _____ and _____ from the west were cut off.

2.76 The battle of Chickamauga was won by the _____ .

2.77 The Union troops retreated to _____ after Chickamauga where they were reinforced by Generals _____ and _____ .

2.78 At the battle of Cold harbor, General Grant lost _____ men the first month.

2.79 General Grant was unable to take _____ although he held the Confederates inside that city for _____ months.

47

2.80   Lincoln was opposed for a second term by _____ .

2.81   Lincoln's vice presidential candidate was _____ .

2.82   Because of Sherman's victory in Atlanta, Lincoln won _____ electoral votes and
         _____ percent of the popular vote for president in 1864.

2.83   Sherman in his march to the sea, left a trail of devastation _____ miles wide and
         _____ miles long.

2.84   Peace talks were held at _____ , Virginia and the surrender took place
         at _____ Court House on April 9, 1865.

Complete this map activity.

2.85   Write the numbers of the Civil War battles listed below at the correct locations on the map.

1. Appomattox
2. Atlanta, GA
3. Bull Run
4. Chattanooga, TN
5. Fort Donelson
6. Fort Sumter
7. Gettysburg
8. Hampton Roads
9. Harper's Ferry
10. Montgomery, AL
11. Port Hudson, LA
12. Potomac River
13. Savannah, GA
14. Vicksburg, MS

Important
Civil War Sites

Adult Check   _____
                    Initial   Date

Review the material in this section in preparation for the Self Test. This Self Test will
check your mastery of this particular section as well as your knowledge of the previous section.

48

SELF TEST 2

True/False (each answer, 1 point)

2.01 _____ Mississippi was the first state to secede from the Union.

2.02 _____ The first battle fought after Fort Sumter was the battle at Manassas Junction.

2.03 _____ Appomattox Court House was the site of one of the worst battles of the Civil War.

2.04 _____ The *Monitor* defeated the *Merrimac* at Hampton Roads in the war's first naval battle.

2.05 _____ General George McClellan was Lincoln's Democratic opponent in the 1864 election.

2.06 _____ Small southern farmers supported the slave system.

2.07 _____ The nation's fastest growing cities in 1850 were in the west.

Choose one answer (each answer, 2 points).

2.08 Which minority wielded greatest political power in its region in the period before the Civil War?
_____ a. farmers in the Northeast
_____ b. planters in the South
_____ c. laborers in the industrial cities
_____ d. ship owners in New England

2.09 The main reason Southerners opposed the election of Abraham Lincoln was:
_____ a. his stand on the protective tariff.
_____ b. his strong Union sentiments.
_____ c. his opposition to expanding slavery.
_____ d. his push toward immediate abolition of slavery.

2.010 Which military advantage was not held by the North?
_____ a. abundant available manpower
_____ b. adequate industrial capacity
_____ c. superior military leaders
_____ d. adequate transportation facilities

2.011 Which statement about General Robert E. Lee is *not* true?
_____ a. He was a wealthy slave owner.
_____ b. His loyalty was divided between his state and the Union.
_____ c. His home state was Virginia.
_____ d. He was victorious in the Seven Day's battle and in the second battle of Bull Run.

2.012 Lincoln resisted the calls to relieve General Grant of command after:
_____ a. Vicksburg.
_____ b. Shiloh.
_____ c. Fort Donelson.
_____ d. Chickamauga

Match these men with their descriptions (each answer, 2 points).

2.013 _____ Jefferson Davis   a. killed by one of his own men

2.014 _____ "Stonewall" Jackson   b. president of the Confederacy

2.015 _____ David Farragut   c. Union general, trained his troops thoroughly

2.016 _____ Joseph Crittenden   d. Lincoln's vice president for his second term

2.017 _____ Andrew Johnson   e. proposed a compromise that was rejected by Lincoln

2.018 _____ George B. McClellan   f. crossed Confederate lines to capture New Orleans

2.019 _____ Robert Anderson   g. Confederate general at first battle of Bull Run

2.020 _____ Alexander Stephens   h. met and defeated Robert E. Lee at the battle of Gettysburg

2.021 _____ General George Meade   i. Confederate vice president

2.022 _____ P.G.T. Beauregard   j. stationed at Fort Sumter at the beginning of war

Fill in the blanks (each answer, 3 points).

2.023   The Confederate capital, _____ , was located in _____ .

2.024   The Union General who assumed command of the army during the last year of the war was _____ .

2.025   Before the Civil War the South thought it would receive assistance from the European countries that needed _____ .

2.026   The Union victories in the summer of 1863 that were the turning point in the war were _____ and _____ .

2.027   Abraham Lincoln first received national attention when he debated with _____ in his campaign for the senate.

2.028   Cutting the Confederacy from east and west as well as north and south was the Union strategy of _____ .

III. RECONSTRUCTION

The terrible war was over. Now the country had to decide how to restore the seceded states, what to do with the new black citizens and how to rebuild the battle-torn South.

SECTION OBJECTIVES

Review these objectives. When you have completed this section, you should be able to:

4. Identify the leading personalities of the Civil War era and explain the consequences of their actions.
8. Outline effects of the war on the North and the South.
9. Examine the Reconstruction efforts made after the Civil War.
10. Recognize that God is no respecter of persons and that we are all equal in His sight.

VOCABULARY

Study these words to enhance your learning success in this section.

enfranchisement	To admit to citizenship
habeas corpus	An order to bring a person before a court to find whether or not he is being held lawfully
impeachment	Charge of misbehavior in office against a government official
literacy test	Test required to indicate the ability of a person to read and write English or to present evidence, such as a school diploma, of his ability to read and write
poll tax	A money payment, usually one or two dollars, required of a person before he could vote; common in the Southern states
Republican radicals	A group in Congress that wished to deal harshly with the defeated South

NORTHERN INFLUENCES

The Civil War preserved the Union, freed the slaves, settled the question of secession, and established the supremacy of federal power; but in the wake of the terrible battles lay the devastation of the South. Almost all of the battles had been fought on Confederate territory. Now the land lay barren, and the social and economic systems were all but destroyed. Poverty and despondency stalked the citizens of the South, and four million freedmen looked to the government for help.

God wanted people to turn to Him. Second Chronicles 7:14 states, "If my people, which are called by my name, shall humble themselves, and pray, and seek my face, and turn from their wicked ways; then will I hear from heaven, and will forgive their sin, and will heal their land." This verse does not mean that God will choose to solve immediately the problems confronting us. However, God provides us with the resources for redemptive healing that will ensue if we do not cling to the negative aspects of our experience.

Faced with the plight of the South, people had the opportunity of pulling together and demonstrating God's principle of forgiveness as they worked to build a stronger nation. However, many people seemed unable to throw off the bitter chains of hatred and retaliation.

President Lincoln. Abraham Lincoln had little military or political experience when he was elected president, but he had firm moral convictions. He consistently pressed toward his goal of holding the Union together, sometimes acting without Congressional approval. Lincoln called for volunteers and expanded the army. He ordered the Union blockade of the South and suspended the writ of **habeas corpus** and imprisoned Southern sympathizers without due process. Lincoln never accepted the possibility of secession; he claimed the Confederate states had never left the Union, that the Union was everlasting.

When Union troops gained control in Tennessee, Louisiana and North Carolina in 1862, Lincoln appointed military governors to reestablish the state governments. He planned to pardon the secessionists who took a prescribed oath of loyalty to the Union. He also planned to recognize representatives of states where 10 percent of the 1860 electorate took the oath and emancipated the slaves in the state.

Some members of Congress opposed Lincoln's plan. They claimed the southern states had severed their ties to the Union and were now reduced to the status of territories. These congressmen proposed the Wade-Davis Bill, which stated that a majority of the electorate had to take the required oath before a state could be readmitted to the Union and that Congress should be responsible for the implementation of the Reconstruction policies.

On April 9 when Lee met Grant at Appomattox, Lincoln was ready to "bind the nation's wounds." However, on Friday April 14, 1865, his hopes and plans were ended by an assassin's bullet as he watched a play in Ford's Theater near the White House. The assassin, John Wilkes Booth, a Southern sympathizer angered by the Confederate defeat, helped to insure a bitter reconstruction period that adversely affected the nation for many years. Lincoln was succeeded by the vice president, Andrew Johnson.

The Freedman's Bureau. The people who were determined to help blacks adjust to freedom and protect their civil rights called for the creation of a department for that purpose. In March of 1865 Congress established the Freedman's Bureau as part of the War Department. Congress initially thought the bureau's work of teaching the freedmen about voting would be completed in a year, but in 1866 a bill was passed that extended the life of one of the United States first social service agencies.

National Archives

John Wilkes Booth

Oliver O. Howard, the chief of the bureau, was interested in more than the **enfranchisement** of black people; he was concerned about their everyday needs. Through Howard's leadership the bureau distributed food to those in need, irrespective of color, and helped provide blacks with clothing, housing, and medicine. The bureau also established schools to educate the black children. However, this action was perceived to be an intrusion of Northern ideas on the Southern culture and was resented almost as much as the voting privileges extended to blacks.

Black Codes. When the slaves were freed, the old slave codes had to be revised. The new codes allowed blacks to swear out affidavits in criminal cases, to sue or be sued in civil courts, and to testify as witnesses during a trial. Marriages between blacks were now sanctioned by law and black children could go to school. The code, however, was restrictive. Blacks could not carry weapons, vote or hold public office, or meet in large groups. In most states white labor was protected by forbidding blacks to work as artisans, mechanics, and in other skilled trades. Strict employment rules bound blacks to their jobs by contract; they were required to be in the regular service of a white person or former owner. In some cases a black person could not be idle without the possibility of being picked up and detained by the state for public work crews without pay.

Southerners saw the new codes as a way to retain their former source of labor. However, in Congress the reports of restrictive codes simulating slavery caused an uproar, and a committee of fifteen was established to investigate conditions in the South.

Constitutional amendments. The Emancipation Proclamation, a war measure designed to encourage the Rebel states to rejoin the Union, could have been declared inoperative at the end of the war. Only those slaves that escaped to the Union lines would have benefited, leaving more than three million slaves in bondage.

Abolitionists and **Republican Radicals** realized that the Emancipation Proclamation needed to be formalized in an amendment to the Constitution that would forever abolish slavery throughout the United States. In December of 1865 the Thirteenth Amendment was ratified by twenty-seven states, some of which were Southern states with provisional governments that had been accepted by Johnson.

In 1866 Congress passed the nation's first Civil Rights Act, overriding the president's veto. This Act granted citizenship to all people born in the United States except Indians.

This new status for the black population was then proposed in the Fourteenth Amendment and sent to the states for ratification. Only one Southern state, Tennessee, ratified the amendment. The second section of the Fourteenth Amendment provided for penalties against any state that did not allow black citizens to vote. At this time only six states in the nation had extended the franchise to all men, and the provision was never enforced.

When Congress saw the effect thousands of blacks had in voting Republicans into office, it proposed the Fifteenth Amendment to provide suffrage for all blacks. Some of the proponents of the bill thought they could sway the black voters and use them to keep their party in office, but others were determined to gain equal rights for all men.

Republican Radicals. Republican Radicals thought the South should be punished. They were unhappy with President Johnson's Reconstruction program, which was modeled after Lincoln's easy terms. Congressman Thaddeus Stevens suggested confiscating the plantations; others wanted forty acres of this land to be given to each former slave. Republican Radicals feared the acceptance of Southern Democrats in Congress would restrict the financial and industrial proposals of their party. They complained that none of the Southern state constitutions provided the right to vote to the black freedmen. Without the black vote, several Republicans thought the South would take the opportunity to elect officials who would return blacks to some system resembling slavery.

Charles Sumner

One of the leaders of the Republican Radicals was Senator Charles Sumner who had been severely beaten in the Senate Chamber during the slavery controversy before the war. He was left an invalid for more than three years by the Southerner who disagreed with Sumner's strong antislavery statements.

In 1867 the Radicals were able to pass the first Reconstruction Act over Johnson's veto. This act removed the Lincoln-Johnson governors already established in the provisional governments and divided all the Confederate states into five military districts. The only exception was Tennessee, which had ratified the Fourteenth Amendment and had been admitted to the Union in 1866. Each of these five districts was governed by an army general who could only be removed when the states held new constitutional conventions that included all male citizens and drew up approved state constitutions. The new state governments were required to guarantee the voting rights of black males and the ratification of the Fourteenth Amendment. Only former Confederates and women were to be excluded from voting.

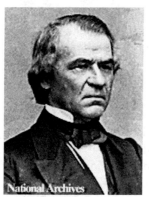

Andrew Johnson

President Johnson. After Lincoln's death, Andrew Johnson, the new president, retained Lincoln's cabinet and planned to follow Lincoln's Reconstruction policy. President Johnson recognized Virginia, Tennessee, Arkansas, and Louisiana under Lincoln's 10 percent plan and pardoned those Confederates who took the oath of allegiance to the Union. He established provisional governments in the other secessionist Southern states and urged the states to ratify the Thirteenth Amendment.

Congress and President Johnson, a previous slave owner and the only senator who had refused to secede with his state, were in conflict on several issues. Johnson's voting record did not support the big plantation owners and he was very sympathetic toward the poor Southerners. Congress did not like the soft Reconstruction policies Johnson advocated. Congress extended the life of the Freedman's Bureau and empowered it to establish schools and help prepare blacks for life as free citizens of the United States. It also proposed the Civil Rights Bill, a measure that guaranteed the basic civil rights of freedmen. Johnson vetoed both measures, but Congress passed both bills over his veto.

Two other measures designed to limit presidential powers were also passed in Congress: (1) the Tenure of Office Act, declaring that the president could not remove federal officials previously approved by the Senate without the Senate's consent, and (2) Command of the Army Act, forbidding the issue of presidential orders to the army without going through the General of the Army.

Ulysses S. Grant

President Johnson defied the Tenure of Office Act and removed Secretary of War Edwin M. Stanton from office. The House immediately called for **impeachment** and tried Johnson in the United States Supreme Court. The presiding justice, Chief Justice Salmon P. Chase, charged Johnson with eleven counts of violating a law of Congress.

Johnson was found innocent, but only one vote separated this decision from the two-thirds necessary for a guilty verdict. The conscientious congressmen who voted "not guilty" were concerned that the nation's system of checks and balances would be destroyed if Congress was able to impeach the president because they were not in agreement.

Johnson retained the presidency but did not run for the office that fall. Ulysses S. Grant won the election with the help of a large black vote in his favor.

Congressional action. Other Reconstruction measures were passed by Congress while Johnson was in office. These measures authorized the military commanders in each of the five southern regions to register voters, supervise elections, appoint and remove state officials, and approve a simple majority for the ratification of proposed state constitutions instead of the two-thirds usually necessary. The Southern states applied for readmittance to the Union under these restrictive guidelines, and all but Mississippi, Texas, and Virginia were readmitted in 1868. The remaining three states were admitted in 1870 along with Georgia, whose original readmittance had been retracted when blacks were expelled from its legislature.

Congressional Reconstruction policies prevented former Confederate soldiers and officials from voting or holding political office. These policies limited the leadership roles to black men, Southerners who had not participated in the war (referred to as "scalawags") and "carpetbaggers" (Northerners who came south after the war to seek political and business opportunities in the South).

During this period, black men were elected to represent their states in the House of Representatives and the Senate. Blanche K. Bruce and Hiram Revels, senators from Mississippi, were joined by fourteen other black officials in Washington, D.C. In the state governments black men served at all levels of government.

Only one state legislature, South Carolina, had a black majority and that only in the lower house. Many of the blacks in office had as much formal education as Southern white people. Blanche K. Bruce had completed his formal education at Oberlin College; Robert Elliot, from South Carolina, was an Eton graduate; and Hiram Revels studied at a Quaker seminary and graduated from Knox College in Illinois.

Protected by military troops, the new legislatures passed some laws beneficial to the South: (1) the elimination of property qualifications for voting in the places where they still existed; (2) reapportionment of state legislatures and representation in Congress; (3) abolishment of debtor's imprisonment; (4) provision of free public schools; and (5) the restoration of the roads, bridges, and factories in the South.

The existence of the "carpetbag" governments was a curse to many Southerners. The Northern carpetbaggers (so-called because they came to the South carrying their belongings in a carpetbag) often influenced the state governments to spend money foolishly. While some money was used wisely for rebuilding roads, constructing schools and other public buildings, much more was wasted. Southerners especially resented illiterate black men voting when experienced white people were banned from office.

Corruption in the carpetbag governments, magnified in the eyes of white Southerners, was in reality a mirror image of corruption in the North during Grant's administration. The Tweed Ring in New York, the Credit Mobilier Scandal, Black Friday, and Grant's mishandling of federal appointments that led to federal civil service reform stole many more dollars from the nation's treasury than any Southern carpetbag government. The discovery of graft by some office holders led Southerners to organize to overthrow the Republican Radicals and to restrict the political activity of black men.

Political compromise. In the 1876 elections the Democratic candidate, Samuel Tilden, received a majority of the popular votes, but only 184 electoral votes; Rutherford B. Hayes, the Republican candidate, received 165 electoral votes. South Carolina, Louisiana and Florida sent in two sets of electoral votes, one set from the "carpetbag" governments still in effect in those states. Hayes needed all the votes from these states and Oregon, which was late getting in its results. Tilden, the Democratic candidate, only needed one of these votes to win the election.

Because of the confusion over the two sets of results, Congress established an Electoral Commission comprised of seven Republicans, seven Democrats and one unbiased justice. However, the unbiased member withdrew from the commission before the election and his replacement was a strong Republican. The eight Republicans voted for Hayes, and he became the nineteenth president of the United States.

The 1877 Compromise was a result of secret talks that assured the South that all federal troops would be removed and that the South would receive money to help build

National Archives

R.B. Hayes (signature)

Rutherford B. Hayes

railroads and factories in return for the acceptance of the presidential election results. The South never received the promised federal financial assistance; however, the troops were removed. The last three states, South Carolina, Louisiana, and Florida, achieved "home rule," and the twelve years of Reconstruction were over.

During Reconstruction most of the white men had regained their political rights by taking the loyalty oath. Many Confederate leaders were pardoned or granted voting rights within seven years; General Lee's voting rights were restored in 1868. Not one Confederate leader was tried for treason or fined for war damages against the Union. Although planters and farmers lost their slaves, they did not lose their lands to the Union government; and military rule lasted only a short time.

SOUTHERN REACTIONS

The end of Reconstruction brought strong reaction from the South and led to the Compromise of 1877 and civil service reform.

Sharecropping and crop-lien systems tied blacks and poor white people to the land without much possibility of improving their living style or increasing their income. The black codes gradually evolved into Jim Crow laws, the Freedman's Bureau was dissolved in 1872 and white opposition to Republican Radical Reconstruction kept the South solidly Democratic for the next one hundred years.

Civil deprivation. Two methods of restricting black involvement in Southern governments were used throughout the South. When black persons could not be coerced into voting the Democratic ticket, they suddenly found they were not able to rent land or receive credit in the stores if they "chose" to vote. These economic measures effectively kept some black men from the voting booth.

Other blacks were frightened by secret groups such as the Ku Klux Klan, Knights of the White Camelia and the White Brotherhood that intimidated black voters and carpetbag officials by threatening physical retaliation. The most renowned of these groups, the Ku Klux Klan, dressed in white hoods and gowns and carried out their activities during the night. They pillaged and burned black churches, homes, schools, and businesses and lynched hundreds of black citizens across the South.

Congress passed the Force Act in 1870 to protect black voters, but by this time many blacks were too frightened to exercise their rights. White Southerners who had been too young for military duty in the Civil War became eligible to vote and helped elect Democratic legislatures. Congress passed the Ku Klux Klan Act in 1871 in an effort to end the reign of terror in some communities. About seven thousand white Southerners were arrested, but few were tried or convicted.

In the North people began to lose interest in the Reconstruction of the South. When a few years of Reconstruction did not erase the effects of two hundred years of slavery, some Northerners began to agree with some Southern white spokesmen that blacks were neither competent nor capable of accepting the responsibilities of citizenship. In 1872 Congress passed the Amnesty Act that made almost all the former Confederates eligible to vote; only five hundred of the highest leaders were still without the voting right.

The Democratic legislatures passed laws that practically eliminated civil rights for black persons. **Poll taxes** and **literacy tests** excluded black men and white men until the "grandfather clause" was enacted. This provision exempted a voter from the literacy test if his grandfather was able to vote by January 1, 1860.

Economic Inversion. The destruction of "the Southern way of life" was caused not by the loss of their slaves, but by the lack of capital, the Union confiscation of Confederate cotton and other property, and federal taxes. These taxes encouraged planters and farmers to enter into the sharecropping and crop-lien systems that eventually depleted the land and lowered prices through overproduction. The resultant poverty added to the devastation started by the war and led to the point where thousands of white farmers lost their land to Northern capitalists and Southern merchants. The resultant drifting away of the white youth from the South led to the idea of the "New South." Blacks would "keep their place" toiling on the land and white people would find work in the new factories and mills. These activities brought a surge of industrialism and segregation to the Southern states.

Complete the matching based on your vocabulary words.

3.1 _____ enfranchisement

a. test required to indicate the ability of a person to read and write English

3.2 _____ habeas corpus

b. a group in Congress that wished to deal harshly with the defeated South

3.3 _____ impeachment

c. charge of misbehavior in office against a government official

3.4 _____ literacy test

d. to admit to citizenship

3.5 _____ poll tax

e. an order to bring a person before a court to find whether or not he is being held lawfully

3.6 _____ Republican Radicals

f. a money payment, usually one or two dollars, required of a person before he could vote

Match these items.

3.7 _____ Wade-Davis Bill

a. assassinated President Lincoln

3.8 _____ Ford Theater

b. required citizens to take oath before readmission as a state

3.9 _____ John Wilkes Booth

c. helped blacks adjust to freedom

3.10 _____ writ of habeas corpus

d. chief of Freedman's Bureau

3.11 _____ Freedman's Bureau

e. suspended by Lincoln

3.12 _____ Oliver O. Howard

f. radical Republican leader

3.13 _____ Charles Sumner

g. site of Lincoln's assassination

Choose the best answer(s).

3.14   What did the new black codes allow the blacks to do?

_____   a. marry by law

_____   b. carry weapons

_____   c. swear out affidavits in criminal cases

_____   d. vote

_____   e. go to school

_____   f. hold public office

_____   g. meets with groups of blacks

_____   h. testify as witnesses during a trial

_____   i. sue or be sued in civil courts

3.15   What were blacks *not* allowed to do according to the codes?

_____   a. marry by law

_____   b. carry weapons

_____   c. vote

_____   d. go to school

_____   e. testify as witnesses during a trial

_____   f. swear out affidavits in criminal cases

_____   g. meets with groups of blacks

_____   h. sue or be sued in civil courts

_____   i. hold public office

3.16   The Civil Rights Act of 1866 granted citizenship to all people born in the United States *except*:

_____   a. Indians

_____   b. Blacks

_____   c. Mexicans

_____   d. Scotch-Irish

3.17   The only Southern state to ratify the Fourteenth Amendment was:

_____   a. Mississippi

_____   b. Alabama

_____   c. Virginia

_____   d. Tennessee

3.18   The act that divided the South into five military districts was the:

_____   a. Sumners Act

_____   b. Reconstruction Act

_____   c. Army Governing Act

_____   d. Civil Rights Act

3.19   The act that prohibited the president from removing federal officials previously approved by the Senate was the:

_____   a. Command of the Army Act

_____   b. Fifteenth Amendment

_____   c. Tenure of Office Act

_____   d. Credit Mobilier Act

3.20   The act that forbade the issue of presidential orders to the army without going through the General of the Army was the:
_____ a. Command of the Army Act
_____ b. Fifteenth Amendment
_____ c. Tenure of Office Act
_____ d. Credit Mobilier Act

3.21   The House of Representatives brought impeachment proceedings against President Johnson because he removed what man from office as Secretary of War?
_____ a. Salmon P. Chase
_____ b. Edwin M. Stanton
_____ c. Ulysses S. Grant
_____ d. Blanche K. Bruce

Fill in the blanks.

3.22   The secret groups in the South that frightened blacks were the _____, the _____ and the _____ .

3.23   The act that protected black voters was the _____ .

3.24   The act that gave former Confederates the right to vote was the _____ .

3.25   Two things that excluded black men and some white men from voting were _____ and _____ .

3.26   In the election of 1876, _____ received the majority of the votes; however, _____ won the election.

Adult Check   _____
                      Initial   Date

Before you take this last Self Test, you may want to do one or more of these self checks.

1. _____ Read the objectives. Determine if you can do them.
2. _____ Restudy the material related to any objectives that you cannot do.
3. _____ Use the SQ3R study procedure to review the material:
   a. Scan the sections.
   b. Question yourself again (review the questions you wrote initially).
   c. Read to answer your questions.
   d. Recite the answers to yourself.
   e. Review areas you didn't understand.
4. _____ Review all activities and Self Tests, writing a correct answer for each wrong answer.

SELF TEST 3

Choose one answer (each answer, 2 points).

3.01 The leading occupation during the 1840s and 1850s was:

_____ a. manufacturing
_____ b. government
_____ c. agriculture
_____ d. shipbuilding

3.02 The most important crop raised in the South was:

_____ a. rice
_____ b. indigo
_____ c. sugar
_____ d. cotton

3.03 The first state to secede from the Union was:

_____ a. Mississippi
_____ b. South Carolina
_____ c. Tennessee
_____ d. Alabama

3.04 Which minority wielded greatest political power in its region in the period before the Civil War?

_____ a. farmers in the Northeast
_____ b. planters in the South
_____ c. laborers in the industrial cities
_____ d. ship owners in New England

3.05 New Orleans was captured by:

_____ a. David Farragut
_____ b. Robert Smalls
_____ c. Robert Anderson
_____ d. Ulysses S. Grant

3.06 The act that divided the South into five military districts was the:

_____ a. Sumners Act
_____ b. Reconstruction Act
_____ c. Army Governing Act
_____ d. Civil Rights Act

3.07 The act that prohibited the president from removing federal officials previously approved by Senate was the:

_____ a. Command of the Army Act
_____ b. Fifteenth Amendment
_____ c. Tenure of Office Act
_____ d. Credit Mobilier Act

Match these men with the appropriate description (each answer, 2 points).

3.08 _____ Abraham Lincoln

3.09 _____ William T. Sherman

3.010 _____ General George McClellan

3.011 _____ Jefferson Davis

3.012 _____ Ulysses S. Grant

3.013 _____ Charles Sumner

3.014 _____ Robert E. Lee

3.015 _____ Stephen Douglas

3.016 _____ P.G.T. Beauregard

3.017 _____ Andrew Johnson

3.018 _____ John Brown

3.019 _____ "Stonewall" Jackson

a. commander of the Union forces

b. radical abolitionist, hanged after an arsenal raid

c. friend of the South and assassination victim

d. led a destructive march across the South

e. president of the Confederacy

f. candidate for the senate in 1860 who debated with Lincoln

g. Lincoln's Democratic opponent in the election of 1864

h. Republican Radical who was savagely beaten

i. commander of the Confederate forces

j. killed by one of his own men

k. led the attack on Fort Sumter

l. escaped impeachment by one vote

Fill in the blanks (each answer, 3 points).

3.020 The Civil War began in _____ and ended in _____ .

3.021 The Wade-Davis Bill required the majority of the electorate to take an _____ before a state could be _____ to the Union.

3.022 General Lee surrendered to General Grant at _____ , Virginia.

3.023 President Lincoln was assassinated by _____ at _____ .

3.024 President Lincoln was replaced by _____ .

3.025 Codes that allowed black people certain freedoms or placed restrictions on them after the Civil War were called _____ .

3.026 The first Southern state to approve the Fourteenth Amendment and be readmitted to the Union was _____ .

Match these items (each answer, 2 points).

3.027 _____ Thirteenth Amendment   a. violated by President Johnson

3.028 _____ Freedmen's Bureau   b. first land battle of the Civil War

3.029 _____ Fort Sumter   c. divided the South into five military districts

3.030 _____ Fourteenth Amendment   d. abolished slavery

3.031 _____ Gettysburg   e. established schools and helped freed slaves

3.032 _____ Compromise of 1877   f. made freedmen U.S. citizens and granted them the right to vote

3.033 _____ Antietam   g. Lincoln dedicated a cemetery here

3.034 _____ Tenure of Office Act   h. bloodiest single-day battle in the Civil War

3.035 _____ poll tax and literacy test   i. required in order for freedmen to vote

3.036 _____ Manassas Junction   j. began the Civil War

3.037 _____ Reconstruction Act   k. removed federal troops from the South

72 / 90

Score
Adult Check

       Initial   **Date**

Before you take the LIFEPAC Test, you may want to do one or more of these self checks.

1. _____ Read the objectives. Determine if you can do them.
2. _____ Restudy the material related to any objectives that you cannot do.
3. _____ Use the SQ3R study procedure to review the material.
4. _____ Review all activities and Self Tests and LIFEPAC Glossary.
5. _____ Restudy areas of weakness indicated by the last Self Test.